AF581208

COMPLETE COLLECTOR'S GUIDE

TO THE ROLLEI TLR

BY
IAN PARKER

LISTING ALL KNOWN ROLLEI TLR CAMERAS 1928 - 1994

AN ORIGINAL FROM **HOVE FOTO BOOKS**

Published October 1993
by
Hove Foto Books Ltd.
Jersey Photographic Museum, Hotel de France
St. Saviour's Road, St. Helier, Jersey, Channel Islands JE2 7LA
Tel: (0534) 73102 Fax: (0534) 35354

Typesetting & Layout : Jersey Photographic Museum

Printed by
The Guernsey Press Co. Ltd., Commercial Printing Division,
Guernsey, Channel Islands

British Library Cataloguing-in-Publication Data
A catalogue record for this book is available from the British Library

Parker Ian -
Collector's Guide to the Rollei TLR

ISBN : 1-874031-95-9

Worldwide Distribution:

Newpro (UK) Ltd.
Old Sawmills Road,
Faringdon, Oxon,
SN7 7DS
Tel:(0367) 242411
Fax:(0367) 241124

CONTENTS

	Page No.
Introduction	4
Pre-War Zeiss Lens Numbers	5
Baby Rolleiflex	6
Rolleicord	23
Special Rolleicord - Models	65
Pre-War Rolleiflex	69
Studio Camera	78
Post-War Rolleiflex	79
3.5F Rolleiflex	107
2.8f Rolleiflex	117
2.8FRolleiflex	137
2.8f Limited Edition	143
2.8 GX Series	147
2.8 GX Rolleiflex Prototypes	149
Rollei Tele & Wide-Angle TLR	153
Rollei Magic TLR	159
Index	165
Jargon Buster	168
Club Rollei	172
Second-Hand Prices	175

INTRODUCTION

Throughout the world can be seen many photographers who regularly use the Rollei TLR camera, in most instances the later F3.5 and F2.8, but surprisingly for those not aware of the superb build quality of Rollei products, many 1930's Rollei TLRs are still in active use today.

The original idea of the TLR was born in 1916. Reinhold Heidecke, the inventor, had to wait until 1927 before the first prototype was completed and it was not until 1929 that the first Rolleiflex TLR went into production.

Rolleiflex or Rolleicord TLR cameras can still be bought at modest cost from those dealers who deal in second-hand cameras. These strongly constructed manual cameras, which are easily repairable, are a joy to hold and use, and so it is understandable why so many collectors spend hours searching for those cameras not in their collection.

This guide should help to identify the many varieties, date of manufacture, and also help to ascertain filter and accessory sizes.

I am sure that there are some Rollei TLR camera numbers outside the range given and I would appreciate any information that will help to update future editions of this guide.

Ian Parker

ACKNOWLEDGEMENTS

The Author would like to thank the assistance given by members of the Jersey Photographic Museum (which owns one of the world's largest collections of Rollei cameras and accessories), and also the help of Club Rollei members and the many who answered pleas for help in the world's photographic Press that enabled some of the hitherto unknown cameras to be included in this guide. Irwin Smoler's (of the USA) listing of the Baby Rollei TLR was also exceedingly helpful.

A big thank you too to those who, both past and present, work with Rollei Fototechnic and who helped with archive material, with special thanks to Herr Dietmar Kanzer, Wolfgang Saß and Claus Prochnow. To all of you - a very big thank you!

A QUICK ROUGH GUIDE TO DATE YOUR PRE-WAR ROLLEI

Pre-War Manufacturing dates of lenses:
(**Note:** Lenses may be retained in stock for two or three years before installation in a camera.)

Year	Carl Zeiss Jena No.
Jan. 1, 1928	903,096
Jan. 1, 1929	919,794
Jan. 1, 1930	922,488
Jan. 1, 1931	1,239,699
Jan. 1, 1932	1,364,483
Jan. 1, 1933	1,436,671
Jan. 1, 1934	1,500,000
Jan. 1, 1935	1,615,764
Jan. 1, 1936	1,674,882
Jan. 1, 1937	1,930,150
Jan. 1, 1938	2,267,991
Jan. 1, 1939	2,527,999

Pre- and Post-War Mirrors:

Another way to date your Rollei. The back of the mirror was stamped with the date of manufacture. Mirrors were not kept in stock for any length of time as the tissue paper contained traces of sulphuric acid - if this became damp the mirror silver would tarnish. Mirrors were delivered each month. Please be careful on removing mirrors as they are easily damaged.

The Baby Rolleiflex

All models of the Baby Rolleiflex, the Standard Rolleiflex and the Rolleicord Twin Lens Reflex camera adopt the same principles: a square format, a reflex viewing screen the exact size of the negative accurately coupled to the taking lens, a between-the-lens shutter, and an eye level or direct vision viewing system. All Rollei cameras are precision built instruments designed for years of trouble free service and it is astonishing indeed to find just how many of the earliest models are still in regular use today. The Rollei optical systems are all sound, well tried formulae, their guiding principal has always been that only the best should be considered good enough for the "Rollei's" as they have come to be affectionately known by the countless thousands of Rolleiflex and Rolleicord devotees.

Before discussing the various characteristics of this camera and its basic operation, first a little about the origins of the Baby Rolleiflex. The first Rollei Twin Lens Reflex, a 6x6 (2¼x2¼) used B1 (117) film or the modern equivalent of 120 size. This camera was introduced into the world markets in January 1929, and became an immediate success. Possibly helped by the gradual demise of the heavy plate camera, and the move to more portable alternatives. The advantage of the Rollei TLR was the viewfinder hood. "What you see is what you get" was the popular advertisement of the day as the viewfinder screen was the exact size of the negative, 2¼x2¼ (6x6cm).

In 1931 Reinhold Heidecke, the Rollei designer, put into production the Baby Rolleiflex, giving superior quality to the 24x36 image of the 35mm. The Baby Rolleiflex in fact gave 38x38mm image size, giving 12 exposures on 127 film.

The birth of the Baby Rolleiflex is interesting from a collector's point of view. One of the complaints on the first Rolleiflex was the poor image seen on the screen. Carl Zeiss endeavoured to design a faster lens than the f3.1 finder lens on the 6x6 TLR, the problem was the even illumination throughout the screen spectrum.

Eventually, Carl Zeiss offered a f2.8 finder lens to Reinhold Heidecke, but this would only cover 38mm of the screen satisfactorily. The additional brightness was such that Wilhelmine, Reinhold Heidecke's wife, suggested a Baby Lady's camera. This gave the impetus to redesign the TLR concept and so the lever wind was born. The lever wind was not easily enlarged for use in the later 6x6 Rolleiflex as the tension obtained by the lever broke or damaged the wind on mechanisation, and therefore the additional cost in providing lever wind on was omitted on the Rolleicord, and from 1957 on the Baby Rolleiflex.

The Baby Rolleiflex was the first Rollei with a f2.8 taking lens with the 1931 f2.8 Tessar option. This small Rollei was sometimes known as the 4x4 or the Rollei sport. Production continued until 1968 with a total output of 570,001 cameras completed. The collector will be interested to hear that there are 12 different models.

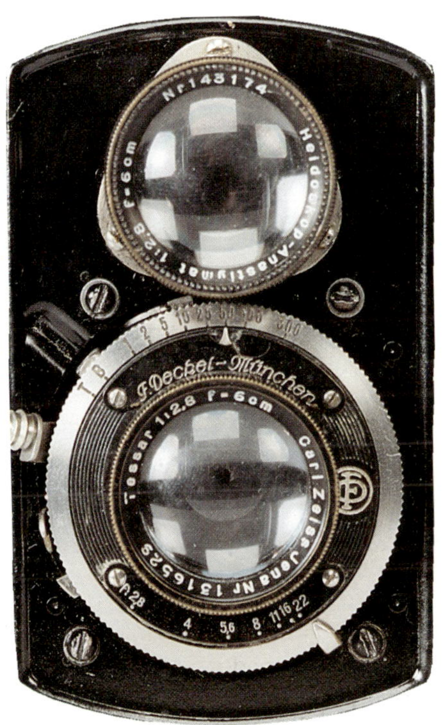

1931 Baby 4x4
The first Rollei to use f2.8 Tessar

Baby 4x4 Rollei TLR

Factory No.	Serial No.		Lens Type	Production Dates
4RF 410	125,000 -	145,000	f3.5	6. 3.1931 - 29.12.1932
4RF 411	125,000 -	145,100	f2.8	6. 3.1921 - 29.12.1932
4RF 413	150,000 -	154,999	f3.5	4. 1.1933 - 6.11.1934
4RF 414	150,000 -	154,999	f2.8	4. 1.1933 - 6.11.1934
4RF 420	155,000 -	523,000	f3.5	1.12.1934 - unknown
4RF 421	155,000 -	523,000	f2.8	1.12.1934 - unknown
4RF 422	155,000 -	524,999	f3.5	unknown - 29.6.1935
4RF 423	155,000 -	524,999	f2.8	unknown - 3. 5.1938
4RF 430	622,000 -	734,999	f2.8	3. 6.1938 - 0. 2.1941
4RF 440	850,000 -	850,999	f2.8	0. 4.1941 - 8.12.1943
K5 Grey	2,000,001 -	2,064,999	f2.8	27. 6.1957 - 0.12.1961
K5 Black	2,065,000 -	2,069,999	f2.8	8. 1.1963 - 30. 5.1963

NOTES AND VARIATIONS:

The above camera numbers are at a variance with those often printed elsewhere. This includes Rollei-Fototechnic current records. A manufacturer would guard their true production figures from competitors which can sometimes make identification difficult. Please note: Model numbers 410 through to 423 all have a front plate combined with shutter and lens assembly, which, by removing 4 screws, enables the cameras to be upgraded. The author would like to hear from anyone who has a 4x4 Rolleiflex with a number that falls outside those set out above to enable any future reprint to be corrected.

Model 410 and 411 are identical except for the lens. They have no exposure guide on the back panel, no peep hole for the shutter speed or the aperture lens setting. The hood catch and the viewing lens mounting are both made out of nickel.

NB: The list facing this page is reprinted from the Club Rollei Magazine. Information from Irwin Smoler (of New York, USA) has helped the author to identify some of the early 4x4 Rollei TLR's.

PRE WAR BABY ROLLEIFLEX (4 X 4) CAMERAS COLLECTION OF IRWIN C. SMOLER

Factory Type	Serial No.	Lens Type	Taking Lens	Viewing Lens	Estimated Year of Manufacture
4RF 410	125001	f3.5	1242534	82825	1931
4RF 410	125022	f3.5	1242022	82557	1931
4RF 410	128621	f3.5	1243608	83067	1931
4RF 410	134542	f3.5	1261639	128911	1931 - 1932
4RF 410 Converted to RF413	138772	f3.5	1238088	142551	1931 - 1932 Converted 1933
4RF 411	138973	f2.8	1337263	132270	1931 - 1932
4RF 411	145068	f2.8	1336790	142266	1932
4RF 414	151375	f2.8	1354095	150643	1933
4RF 413	154366	f3.5	1242490	154660	1933
4RF 421	155881	f2.8	1372481	155805	1934 - 1935
4RF 420	157843	f3.5	1328159	156895	1934 - 1935
4RF 423	522099	f2.8	1878421	504798	1936 - 1937
4RF 423	522558	f2.8	1887934	505456	1936 - 1937
4RF 423	522975	f2.8	1878557	504498	1936 - 1937
4RF 423	523689	f2.8	1987744	505059	1936 - 1937
4RF 430	642372	f2.8	2097332	561400	1938
4RF 430	734536	f2.8	2262862	561400	1939
4RF 440	850029	f2.8	2263262	561295	1941 - 1943
	** 734647	f2.8			

** This camera is experimental with Schneider-Kreuznach Xenotar TA and lens No.3266758 and Schneider-Kreuznach viewing lens No.3266763 - both lenses are coated with Schneider Red Triangle markings.

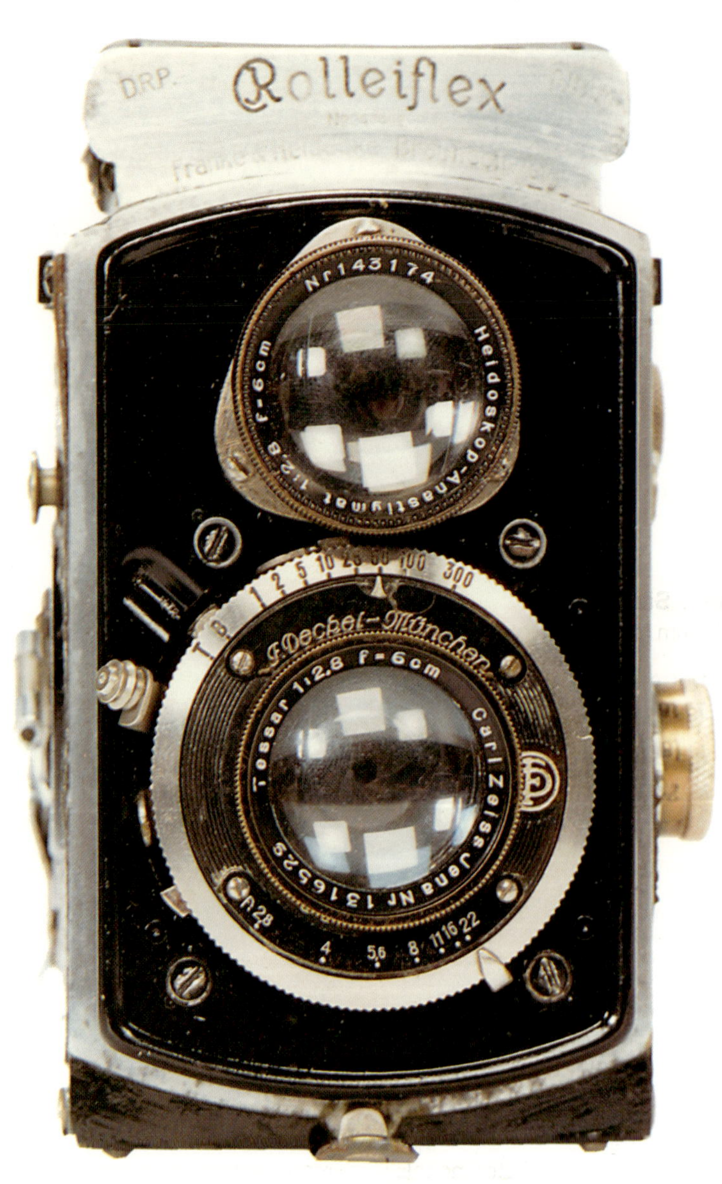

1931 4x4 Rolleiflex
No. 4RF 411
with f2.8 Tessar lens

Baby 4x4 1931 Rolleiflex

Factory Model
4RF 410 / 4RF 411

Launch Date
06-03-1931

Factory Termination Date
29-12-1932

Serial Numbers
125,000 - 145,100

Taking Lens
410 Model f3.5/60mm Tessar
411 Model f2.8/60mm Tessar

Finder Lens
Heidoscop-Anastigmat
f2.8/60mm

Shutter
Deckel Rim Set Compur

Speeds
B, T, 1, 1/2, 1/5, 1/10, 1/25, 1/50, 1/100, 1/300

Filter Size
28.5mm Push-on

Film size
127

Dimensions
10.7 x 7 x 7.5cm

Weight
(410) - 517g (411) - 558g

Launch Price

Germany	(410) RM199	(411) RM219
USA	(410) $78.50	(411) $94
UK	(410) £20	(411) £22.50

Identification

No exposure guide on the back of the camera, no peep hole above the finder lens for shutter and aperture readings. Hood catch and finder lens mounting made of nickel painted black. All Pre-War Baby 4x4 Rollei's had a lever wind.

Variations

Both models 4RF 410 and 4RF 411 are identical except for the Carl Zeiss lens, either f3.5 or f2.8. The larger f2.8 lens (launch date 11-06-1931), increased the weight by 41 grams. Later models were made with depth of focus tables on the rear leaf of the hood.

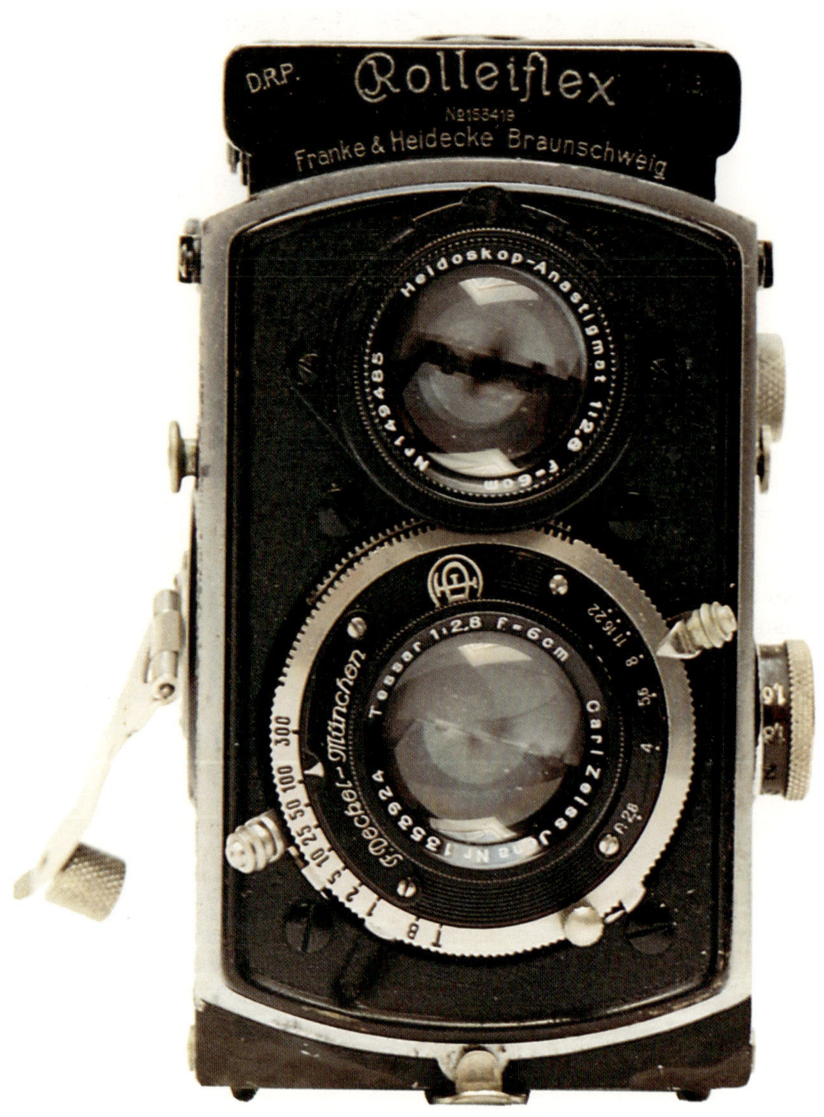

1933 4x4 Rolleiflex
No. 4RF 414
Note taking lens supplied in 1931 - see page 5

Baby 4x4 1933 Rolleiflex

Factory Model
4RF 413 / 4RF 414

Launch Date
04-01-1933

Factory Termination Date
06-11-1934

Serial Numbers
150,000 - 154,999

Taking Lens
(413) f3.5/60mm
(414) f2.8/60mm Tessar

Finder Lens
Heidoscop-Anastigmat
f2.8/60mm

Shutter
Deckel Rim Set Rapid

Speeds
B, T, 1, 1/2, 1/5, 1/10, 1/25, 1/50, 1/100, 1/300

Filter Size
28.5mm Push-on

Film Size
127

Dimensions
10.7 x 7 x 7.5cm

Weight
(420) 517g (421) 558g

Launch Price

Germany	(413)	RM185	(414)	RM200
USA	(413)	$115	(414)	$130
UK	(413)	£21.50	(414)	£23

Identification

Similar to 1931 Baby 4x4 Rolleiflex except for the peep holes above the finder lens for speed and aperture settings which are controlled by levers. Note shutter speed to 1/300th. Later models with top speed 1/500th. Note Compur shutter number below taking lens.

Variations

The exposure scale on the camera back is in different languages. Type 410 and 411 have the aperture and shutter speed range at the top and bottom of the viewing lens whereas on the 413, 414 and later models, they are located on the sides of the taking lens.

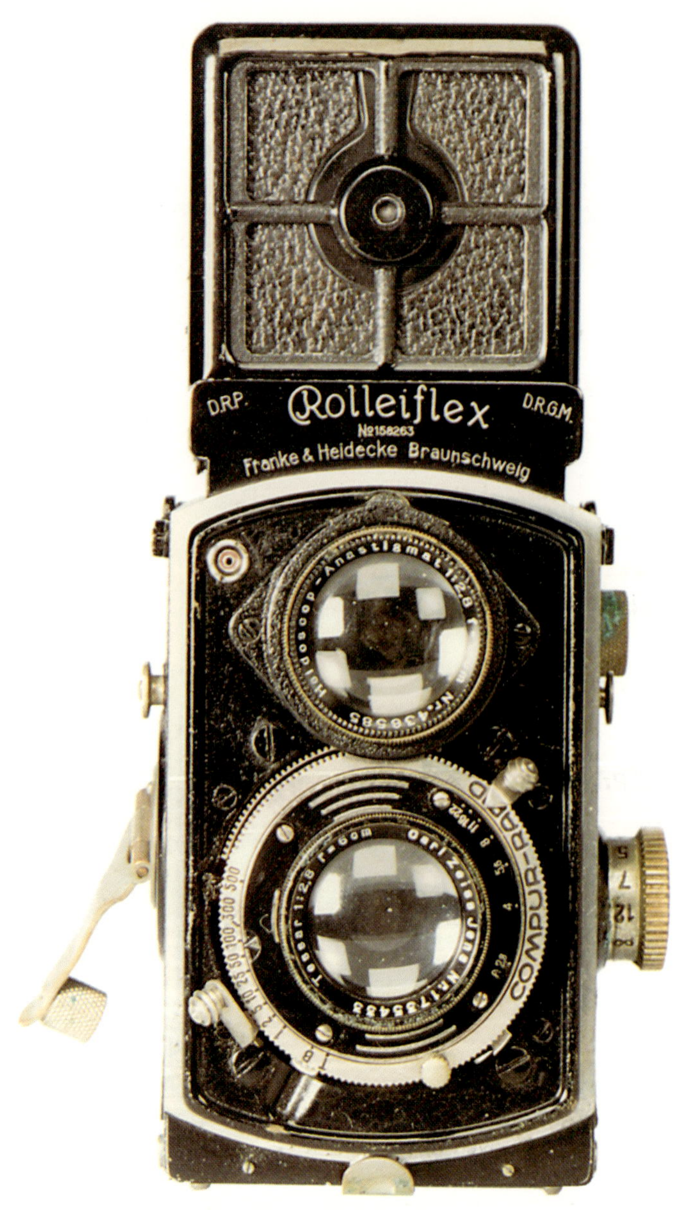

1936 Model 4RF 421 with f2.8 lens
Note shutter speeds

Baby 4x4 1934/7 Rolleiflex

Factory Model
4RF 420 / 4RF 421 /
4RF 422 / 4RF 423

Launch Date
01-12-1934

Factory Termination Date
29-06-1935 (422)
03-05-1938 (423)

Serial Numbers
155,000 - 524,999

Taking Lens
(420&422) f3.5/60mm Tessar
(421) f2.8/60mm Tessar

Finder Lens
Heidoscop-Anastigmat
f2.8/60mm

Shutter
Deckel Compur Rapid

Speeds
B, T, 1, 1/10, 1/25, 1/60,
1/100, 1/250, 1/500

Filter Size
28.5mm Push-on

Film Size
127

Dimensions
10.7 x 7 x 7.5cm

Weight
(422) 567g (423) 583g

Launch Price					
	Germany	(422)	RM185	(423)	RM200
	USA	(422)	$97.50	(423)	$116.50
	UK	(422)	£16.37	(423)	£18.75

Identification
With Compur Rapid shutter to 1/500th. The f3.5 lens model 4RF 422 was discontinued due to poor sales on 29-6-1935 and consequently is sought after by collectors. The 1935 model features a larger focusing knob.

Variations
1934 featured an exposure guide on the back of the camera in different languages. This feature was also introduced on the 6x6 Rolleiflex in 1934. Model Nos. 4RF 420 & 421 have the same shutter as the 1934 6x6 Rolleiflex where the speed sequence ends in 100, 300 & 500. Models 422 & 423 have the automat 6x6 Rolleiflex shutter with end sequence 100, 250 & 500. Model 422 was made to use f3.5 lenses only, which were originally bought for model 420.

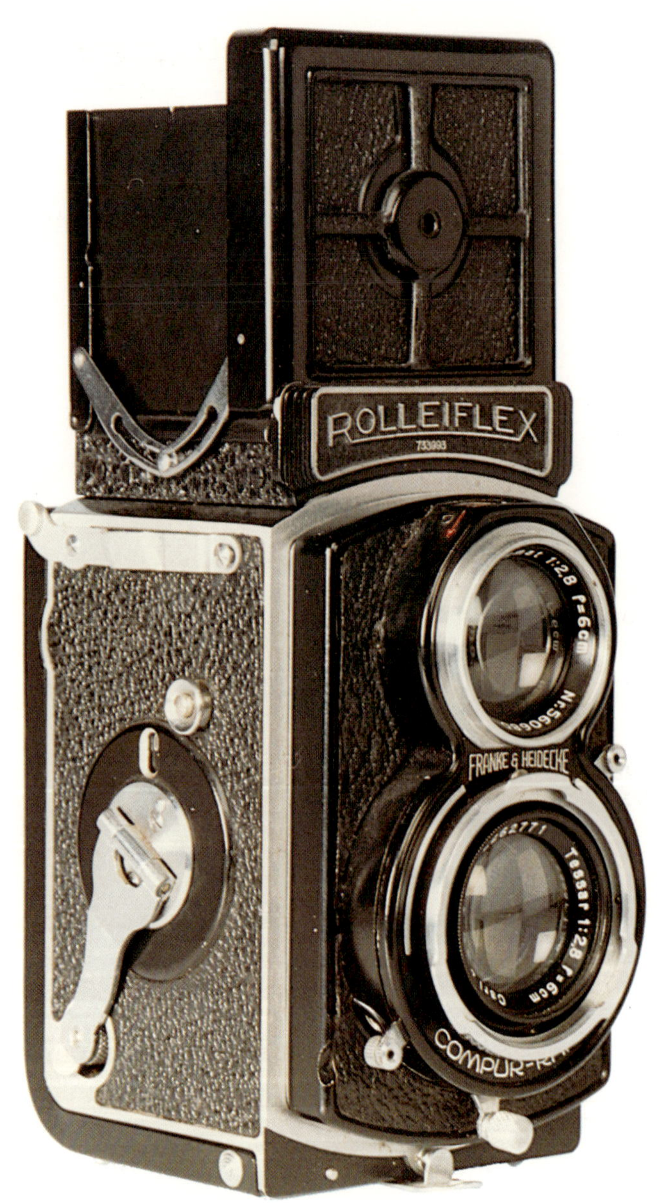

1938 4x4 Model 4RF 430
Also known as Baby Sport

Baby 4x4 1938 Rolleiflex

Factory Model
4RF 430/4RF 440

Launch Date
03-06-1938

Factory Termination Date
08-12-1943

Serial Numbers
(430) 622,000 - 734,999
(440) 850,000 - 850,999

Taking Lens
Carl Zeiss Tessar
f2.8/60mm

Finder Lens
Heidoscop-Anastigmat
f2.8/60mm

Shutter
Deckel
Compur-Rapid

Speeds
B, T, 1, 1/10, 1/25, 1/60, 1/100
1/250, 1/500

Filter Size
Bayonet

Film Size
127

Dimensions
11.3 x 7.5 x 7.9cm

Weight
580g

Launch Price Germany RM200 USA $105 UK £18.95

Identification

First Baby Rolleiflex with Bayonet I on taking lens and cast name plate. All fittings chrome plated - previous models were nickel plated. This camera was given the name "Sport" baby Rolleiflex as a single lever under the taking lens both cocked and released the shutter enabling sequence sports photography.

Variations

Factory model number 4RF 440 is identical to model 430 of which 1000 were manufactured in stages between April 1941 and completed on the 8th December 1943. This camera was only available in Germany.

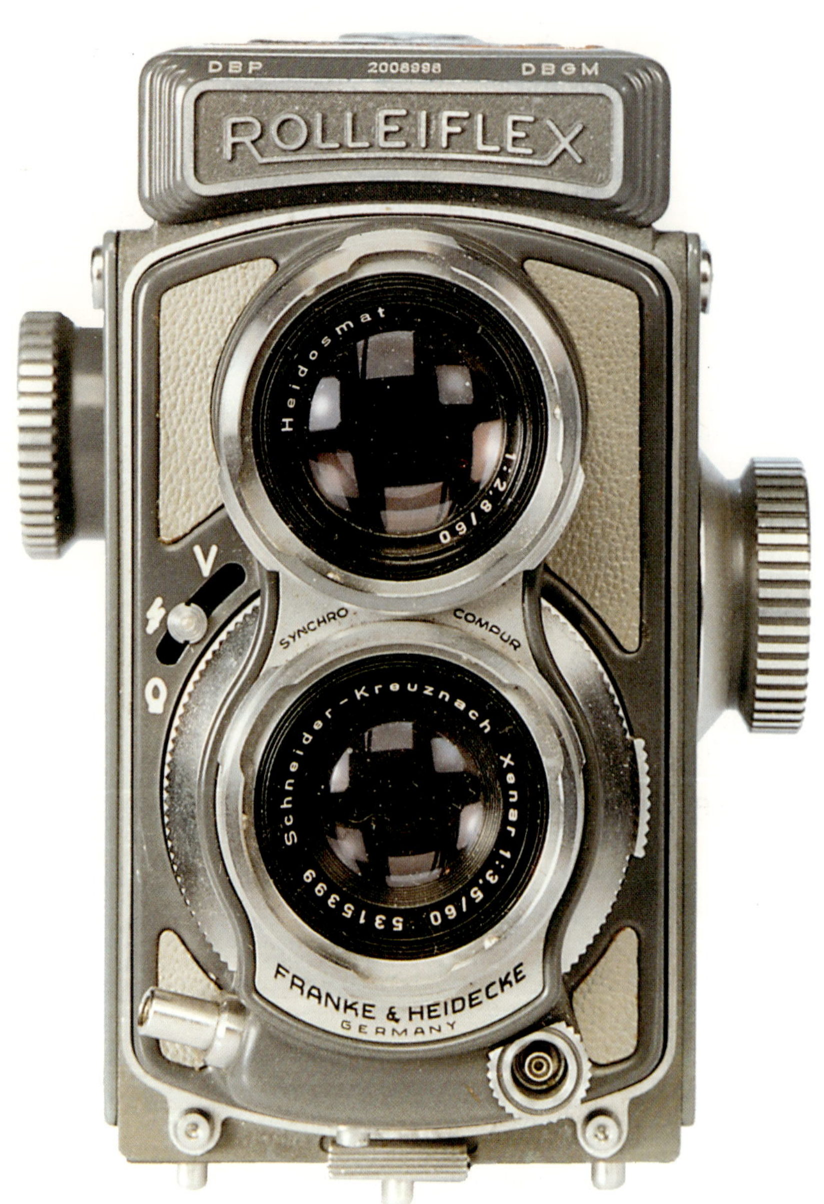

1958 4x4 Model K5 Grey
Note no lever wind

Baby 4x4 1957 Grey Rolleiflex

Factory Model
K5 Grey

Launch Date
27-06-1957

Factory Termination Date
01-12-1961

Serial Number
2,000,001 - 2,064,999

Taking Lens
Schneider Xenar
f3.5/60mm

Finder Lens
Heidosmat
f2.8/60mm

Shutter
Synchro-Compur

Speeds
B, 1, 1/10, 1/25, 1/50, 1/100, 1/250, 1/500

Filter Size
Bayonet I

Film size
127

Dimensions
12.3 x 8.9 x 8.1cm

Weight
700g

Launch Price Germany DM355 USA $133.65 UK £46.30

Identification

This is the only grey baby Rolleiflex with Bayonet I accessory adaptor on both lenses. With a production of 65,000, good clean examples are easily found at a modest cost. A truly delightful, well engineered camera that should be in every Rollei enthusiast's collection.

Variations

The focusing knob is calibrated in feet or metres, thus giving you an excuse for having two of these cameras in your collection. Later production from about No.2,050,600 with same spec. as later black version.

Remarks

1000 grey 4x4 Rolleiflexes were sold to the German Navy with a special metal waterproof case.

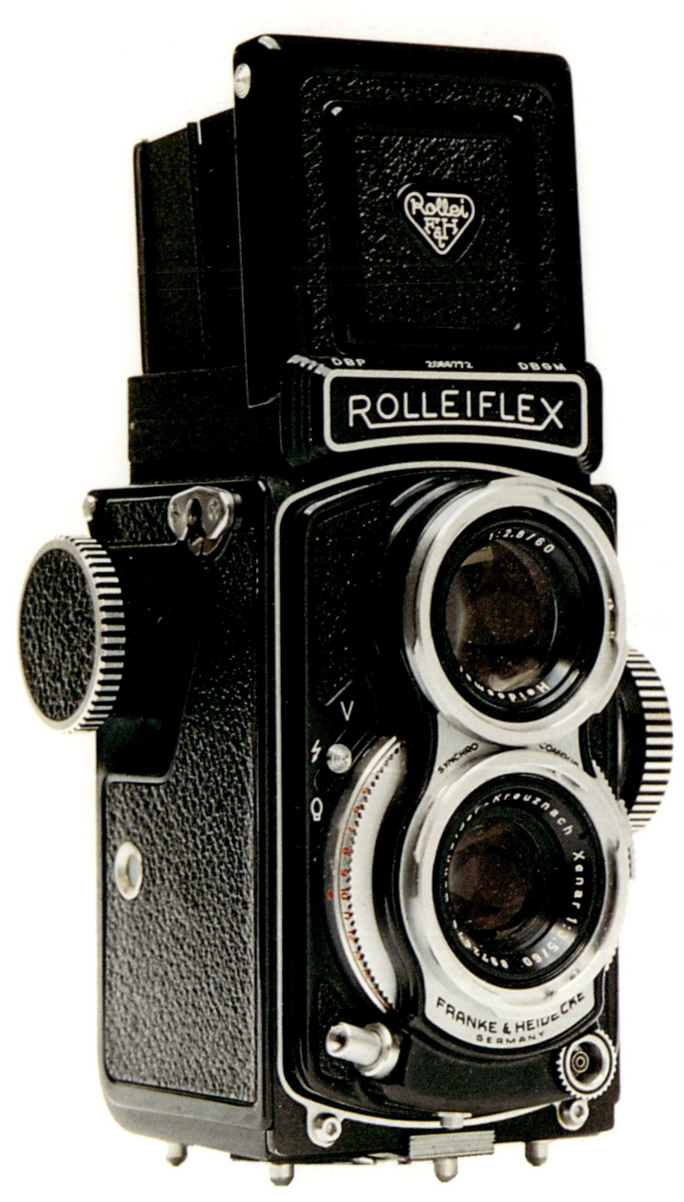

1963 4x4 Model K5 Black
Very collectable

Baby 4x4 1963 Black Rolleiflex

Factory Model
K5 Black

Launch Date
08-01-1963

Factory Termination Date
30-05-1963

Serial Numbers
2,065,000 - 2,069,999

Taking Lens
Schneider Xenar
f3.5/60mm

Finder Lens
Heidosmat
f2.8/60mm

Shutter
Synchro-Compur MXV

Speeds
1-1/500, B

Filter Size
Bayonet I

Film Size
127

Dimensions
12.3 x 8.9 x 8.1cm

Weight
700g

Launch Price Germany DM395 USA $150.00 UK £70.50

Identification
Cosmetically the same as the grey 1957 model. Internally, minor improvements were made to the transportation and safety interlock system. The black leather replaced the grey leather which was prone to shrinkage and colour discolouration, and thereby led to the spoiling of a very collectable camera.

Variations
Only 5000 cameras were manufactured, and, with 127 film costing the same as the 120 size, demand for this camera was not sufficient to be viable. This is a very collectable camera and quite difficult to find! Distance scale in metres or feet.

Remarks
Whether 5,000 cameras were constructed is not known. 5,000 numbered plates were ordered and delivered. With production only lasting 5 months, it is likely that only 3,000 were actually sold. The author would like to hear from anyone who owns a camera with a number above 2,068,000.

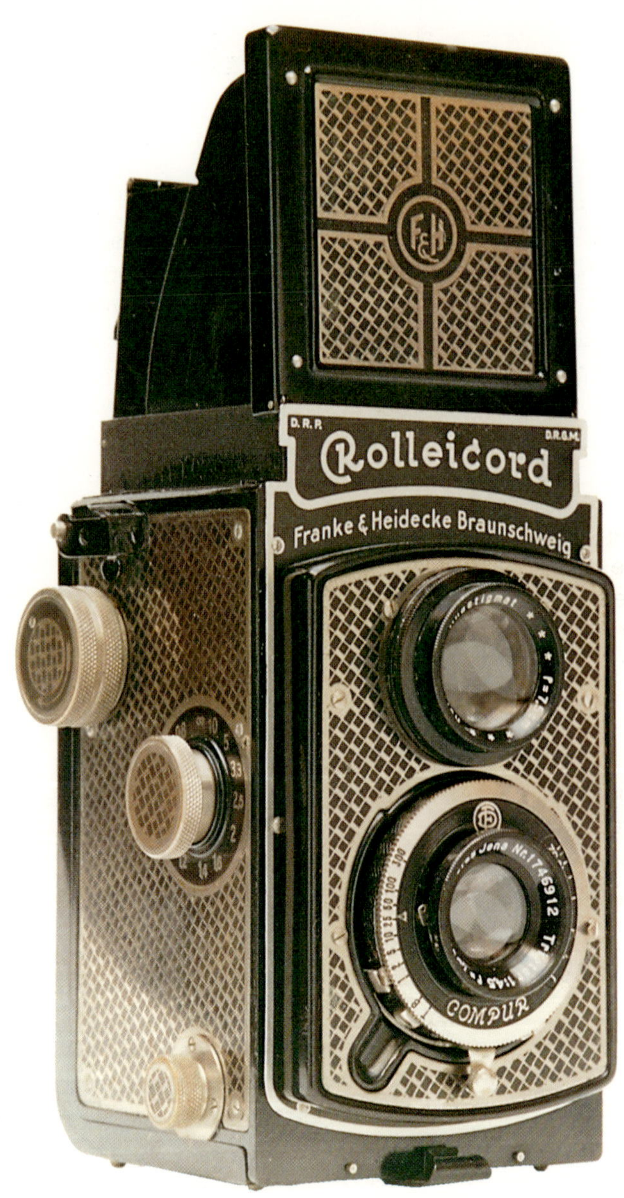

1933 Economy Model
The New Rolleicord

The Rolleicord

Why, in 1933 did Franke & Heidecke introduce the Rolleicord?

In 1932 Heidecke made a prototype twin lens camera with an Art Deco design outer case. At first Paul Franke did not like the design. He was right, as they didn't sell as many of this style as they did of the traditional black finish of the Rolleiflex Stereo and TLR of that period. A comeback was made a year later. Owing to rumours that a competitor was going to market a cheaper TLR, Franke & Heidecke agreed to market the Art Deco as a budget priced Rollei TLR.

The name Rolleicord came about over a dinner held at the Heidecke's house. Paul Franke suggested, after several hours of deliberation, that the camera should incorporate "Cop" from the Heidoscop or Rolleiscop. Heidecke wanted his initials in the name and then his wife Wilhelmine suggested Cord. "Co" from Cop, "R" from Reinhold, and "D" from Deco which in English translates to window dresser. After all, the idea of marketing this camera was that when the two cameras were placed side by side on the photographic shop window it could not be confused with the more expensive Rolleiflex.

So the name Rolleicord came into existence. In November 1933 the "Cord" went on sale in time for Christmas and remained in production until March 1936. Ironically the Art Deco was not popular with a total production of only 11,600. The camera was sold in 1934 in Germany for RM88. An identical model in black, which was cheaper to construct, was sold for RM105. Many bought the black version which resembled a Rolleiflex that cost RM192.

Throughout the Rolleicord line of cameras the Rolleicord has always had a lens which is inferior to the Rolleiflex. From 1949 it was possible to obtain the Rolleicord with a Schneider 4 element lens. The Xenar, for all practical purposes, was identical to the Zeiss 4 element Tessar. The Tessar for that period was available on the Rolleiflex, the Rolleicord and 3.5 Rolleiflex until it was replaced by the Planar or Xenotar lens which gave identical results.

The other lens available for the Rolleicord was the Zeiss Triotar, a three element lens, which although an able performer was not as good as the Xenar. I have heard it said by many photographic dealers that the Rolleicord with the Zeiss Triotar is a better camera than the Xenar version, which is not true.

I can recommend all those that are looking for a reasonably priced TLR camera to use the Rolleicord with the Xenar Lens. It is a superb, well built camera, which is easily repaired and should give many years of service. Collectors tend to pass by the Cord and therefore prices are reasonable and cameras in almost mint condition are not hard to find.

The Rolleicord's film wind-on was by a knob which could be less troublesome than the Flex lever wind: pre-war film would not wind as easily as today's plastic coated backing paper. Up until 1950 you had to position the film, winding on by looking through the red window at the numbers printed on the film's backing paper. The Rolleicord III system is exactly the same as today's Rolleiflex 2.8GX. You line up the arrow on the film's backing paper to the red marks located either side of the film channels. This model saw the introduction of lens coating and flash factory fitted shutter synchronization.

For the collector to assess the age of a Rolleicord, the camera number is the best guide. Many early cameras were altered, upgraded with added flash synchronization, a large "Do It Yourself" focus knob, and an adjustable pressure plate back was fitted. I have seen Rolleicords with a Zeiss 3.5f Tessar, the lens taken from a Rolleiflex and they are both the same physical size.

Rolleicord prototypes are rare. Any prototype would be given to the tooling department in order to obtain quotations and then order the cameras. The research and design section concentrated their efforts on the Rolleiflex. When a new model was put into production the older Flex was looked at to see if any improvements could be used on the Cord. No Cord was fitted with a light meter. The Cord was a simple and trouble free camera.

See note on early Rolleicord serial numbers on page 164.

The Rolleicord 6x6 TLR

Serial numbers	Model No.	Factory Type	Year	Page No.
Nos. On Taking lens:				
1,460,000 - 1,759,000	I	(5RC 510)	1933	27
1,590,000 - 1,759,999	I	(5RC 511)	1934	29
1,760,000 - 1,947,000	Ia	(5RC 520)	1936	31
1,758,000 - 1,973,999	II	(5RC 521)	1936	33
1,945,000 - 2,183,000	Ia2	(5RC 530)	1937	35
1,966,000 - 2,124,000	IIa	(5RC 540)	1937	37
Nos. on Name Plate:				
611,000 - 1,042,999	Ia3	(5RC 531)	1938	39
612,000 - 858,999	IIb	(5RC 541)	1938	41
859,000 - 1,006,999	IIc	(K3 542)	1939	43
1,007,000 - 1,134,999	IId	(K3 543)	1949	45
1,135,000 - 1,135,999	IIe	(K3 544)	1949	47
1,137,000 - 1,344,050	III	(K3 B)	1950	49
1,344,051 - 1,390,999	IV	(K3 C)	1952	51
1,500,000 - 1,583,999	V	(K3 D)	1954	53
1,584,000 - 1,599,999	Va	(K3 E)	1957	55
1,900,000 - 1,943,999	Va2	(K3 Ea)	1958	57
2,600,000 - 2,649,999	Vb	(K3 F)	1962	59
2,650,000 - 2,665,999	Vb2	(K3Fa)	1970	61
2,666,000 - 2,677,498	Vb3	(K3Fb)	1971	63
End of production			1976	

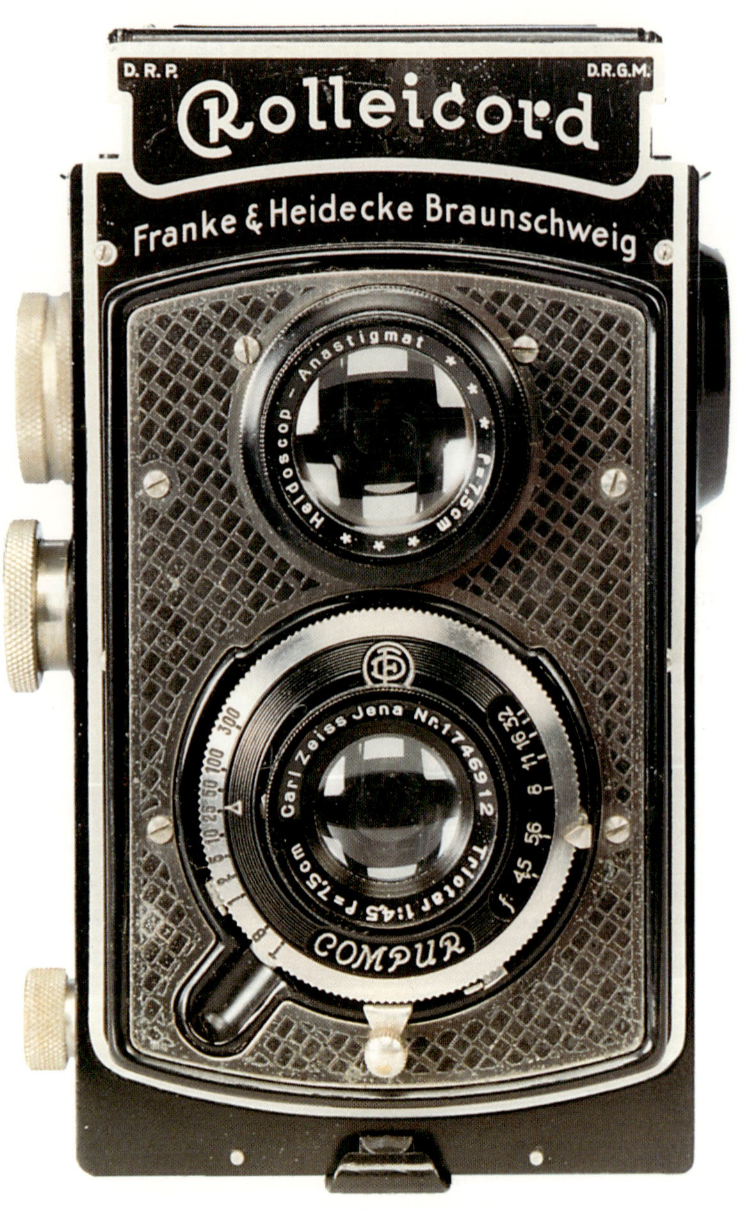

1936 Rolleicord Art Deco
This unused example - A collector's dream!

Rolleicord Art Deco

Factory Model
Number 5RC 510

Launch Date
November 1933

Factory Termination Date
March 1936

Serial Numbers
1,460,000 - 1,759,000 Located on Taking Lens

Taking Lens
Carl Zeiss Triotar
f4.5/75mm

Finder Lens
Heidoscop-Anastigmat
f4/75mm

Shutter
Deckel Rim Set Compur

Speeds
1-1/300, B, T

Filter Size
28.5mm Push-on

Film Size
120 or 35mm with Rolleikin

Dimensions
13.4 x 8.2 x 9.2cm

Weight
863g (31oz)

Launch Price Germany RM88 USA $58 UK £11.75

Identification
This is the only Rollei where the body panels are covered with a diamond patterned metal Art Deco design. With external frame counter, rim set shutter with speeds T, B, 1, 1/2, 1/5th, 1/10th, 1/25th, 1/50th, 1/100th and 1/300th, and a three element Carl Zeiss Jena Triotar lens.

Variations
Non removable or removable back was supplied for fitting a Rolleikin 35mm or a plate back. Backs with exposure guide and depth of field scales are available in English or German. Two types of strap holder: a "peg" at the bottom middle of the camera sides, and later the camera strap passed through a metal loop and hooked onto a metal downward pointing spur. The original camera art deco panels were engraved and nickel plated, these were later brass plated. The early models had no provision for removing the back to fit a plate back or Rolleikin for 35mm film. Some English versions have black leather panel covers for the focusing, wind on and spool knobs.

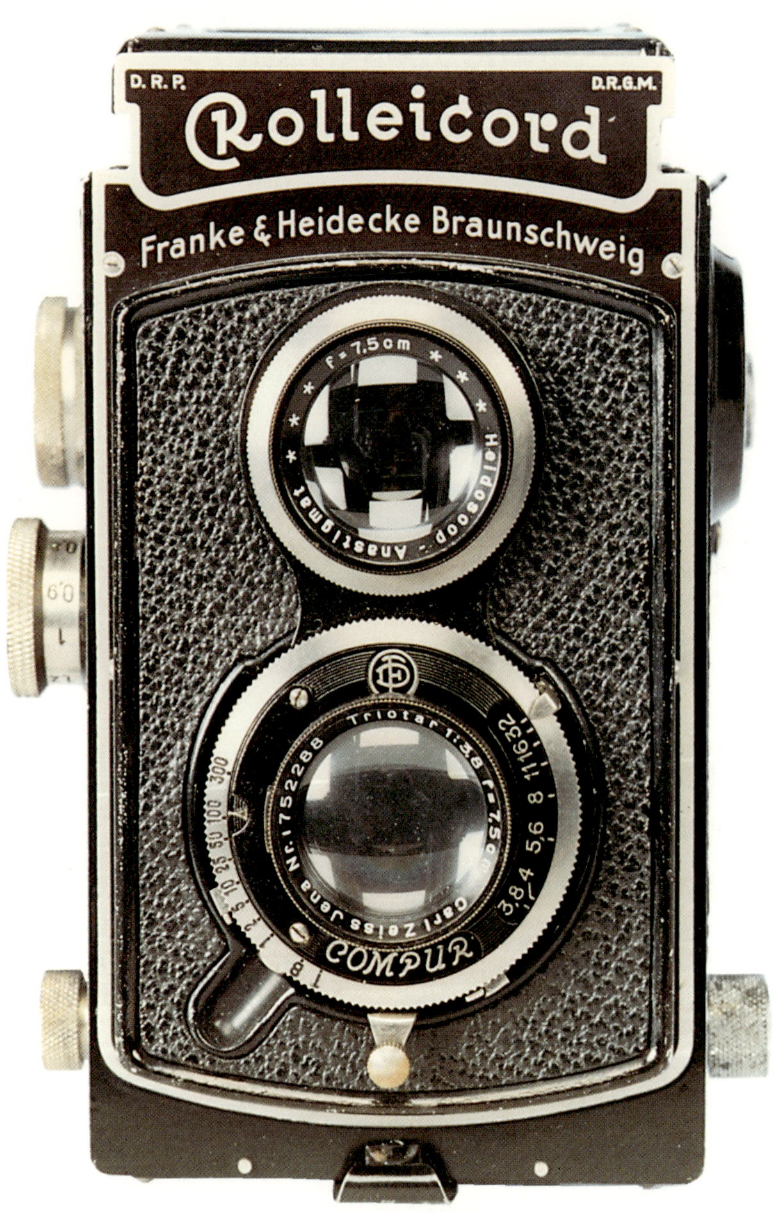

1936 Model 5RC 511
Similar to Art Deco

Rolleicord Model I

Factory Model
5RC 511

Launch Date
00-12-1934

Factory Termination Date
00-08-1936

Serial Numbers
1,590,000 - 1,759,999
On Taking Lens

Taking Lens
Carl Zeiss Triotar
f3.8/75mm

Finder Lens
Heidoscop-Anastigmat
f4/75mm

Shutter
Deckel Rim Set Compur

Speeds
T, B, 1, 1/2, 1/5, 1/10, 1/25, 1/50, 1/100, 1/300

Filter Size
28.5mm Push-on

Film Size
120 or 35mm with Rolleikin

Dimensions
13.4 x 9.3 x 9.5cm

Weight
818g (29oz)

Launch Price Germany RM105 USA $57.50 UK £14.50

Identification

The only Rolleicord with a f3.8 taking lens similar to Art Deco model, but is covered with black leather with no exposure guide or depth of field scales. Camera body number located in film chamber. Numbers, it is said, relate to invoice number rather than camera number.

Variations

Additional external two spool holders on counter side. There is a small handle on the Aperture lever found on salesmen's and distributors' sample cameras which allowed fast hand bracketing. The additional cost did not allow this refinement in final production, when the price in the UK was reduced to £13.75.

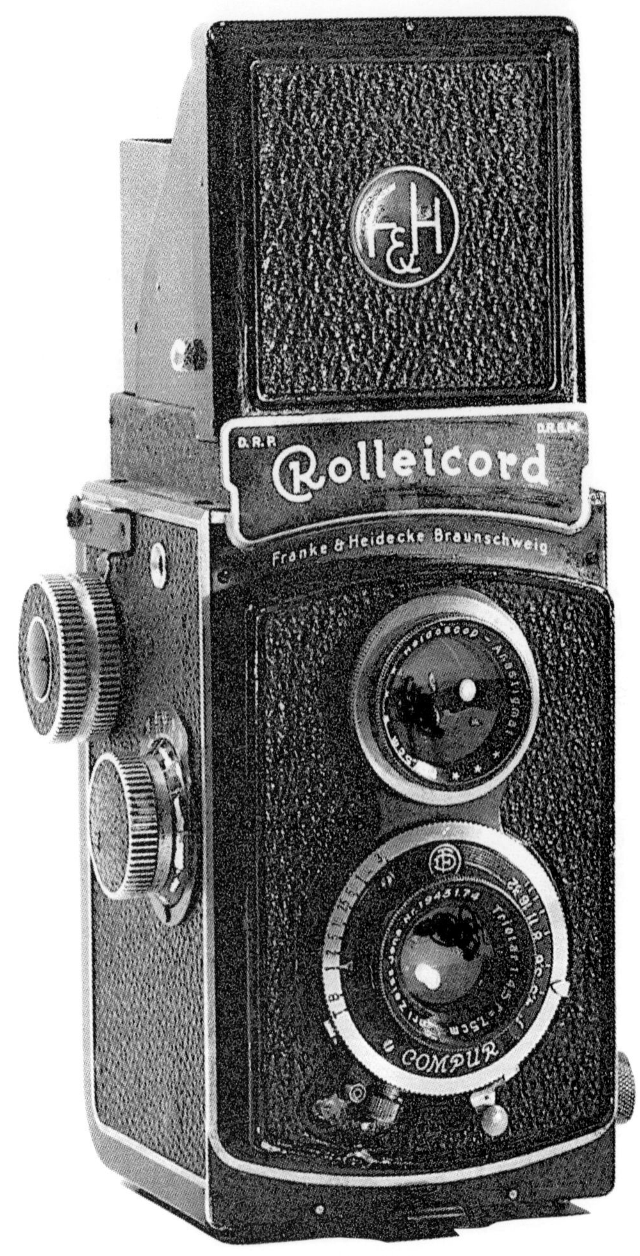

All colour camera photographs taken from the collection in the Jersey Photographic Museum. Our Rolleicord 1a is on loan to a museum in France

Rolleicord Model Ia

Factory Model
5RC 520 Model 1a

Launch Date
22-02-1936

Factory Termination Date
02-08-1937

Serial Numbers
1,760,000 - 1,947,000
On Taking Lens

Taking Lens
Carl Zeiss Triotar
f4.5/75mm

Finder Lens
Heidoscop-Anastigmat
f4/75mm

Shutter
Deckel Rim Set Compur

Speeds
T, B, 1, 1/2, 1/5, 1/10, 1/25, 1/50, 1/100, 1/300

Filter Size
28.5cm Push-on

Film Size
120 or 35mm with Rolleikin

Dimensions
13.4 x 9 x 9.5cm

Weight
811g (28oz)

Launch Price Germany RM96 USA $75 UK £16.50

Identification

No sports finder in redesigned hood with a mirror for eye-level viewing. f4.5 Triotar lens, etched name plate as on previous models. No exterior film counter; a window above focusing knob reveals internal counter. Camera bodies no longer numbered as on previous models. With this model semi-automatic film winding was started. By setting the first frame to No.1 in the red window, thereafter the film came to a definite stop for each frame. This model featured a large eye-level focusing magnifier, it was more ornamental than useful.

Variations

Exposure guide on back in various languages that includes German, English, French and Spanish. Focusing knob calibrated in metres or feet. With or without F&H logo on hood.

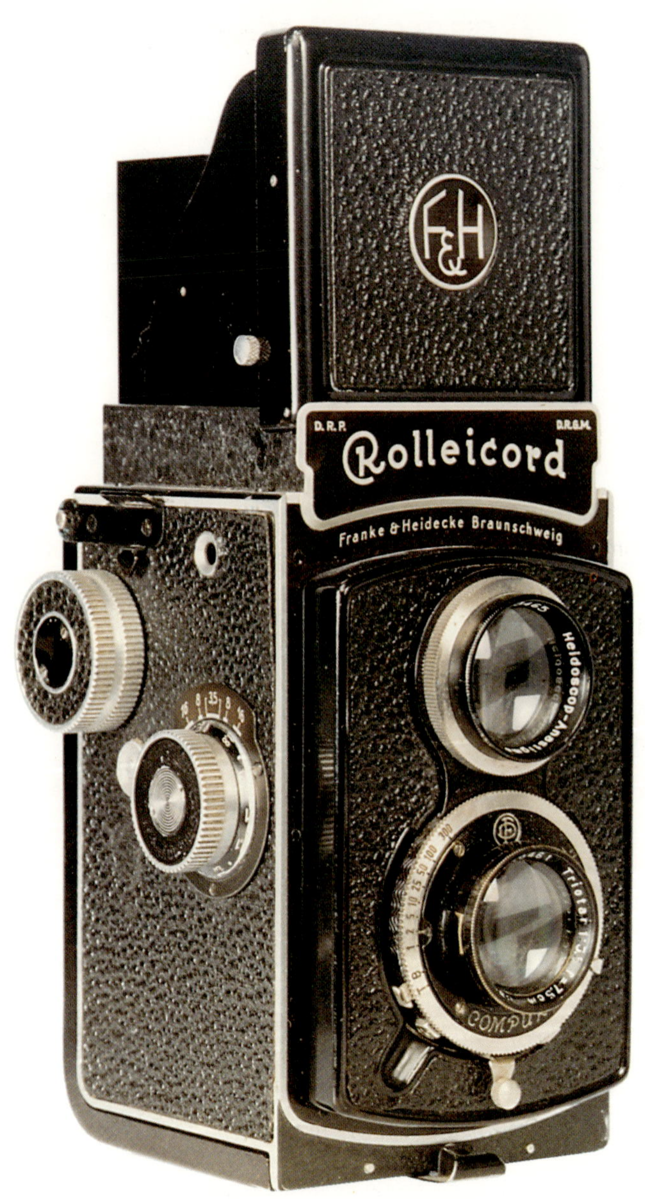

1937 Rolleicord II
No. 5RC III 521 Model 3.5

Rolleicord Model II

Factory Model
5RC III 521 Model 3.5
Rolleicord II

Launch Date
22-02-1936

Factory Termination Date
02-08-1937

Serial Numbers
1,758,000 - 1,973,999
On Taking Lens

Taking Lens
Carl Zeiss Triotar
f3.5/75mm

Finder Lens
Heidoscop-Anastigmat
f3.2/75mm

Shutter
Deckel Compur Rim Set

Speeds
T, B, 1, 1/2, 1/5, 1/10, 1/25,
1/50, 1/100, 1/300

Filter Size
28.5mm Push-on

Film Size
120 or 35mm with Rolleikin

Dimensions
13.4 x 9.4 x 9.6cm

Weight
793g (28oz)

Launch Price Germany RM128 USA $80 UK £18.75

Identification

Only Rolleicord with f3.5 lens and push on filter. Later f3.5 Cords accepted Bayonet I filters and accessories. Name plate etched with Rolleicord name with smaller lettering for "Franke & Heidecke Braunschweig" compared to previous models. Hood has larger 18mm eye-level focusing lens, previous models had 13mm, but with no eye-level sports finder.

Variations

Hood with or without F&H Logo. Exposure guide on camera back in various languages. Most common, English & German. Please note the f4.5 model of this camera is Model No. 5RC 530 1a. The internal screws may be nickel plated or black. The distance scale on the focusing knob is in metres. The black paint is easily scratched off leaving a bright nickel ring. Alas no information as to the working of the depth scale is available.

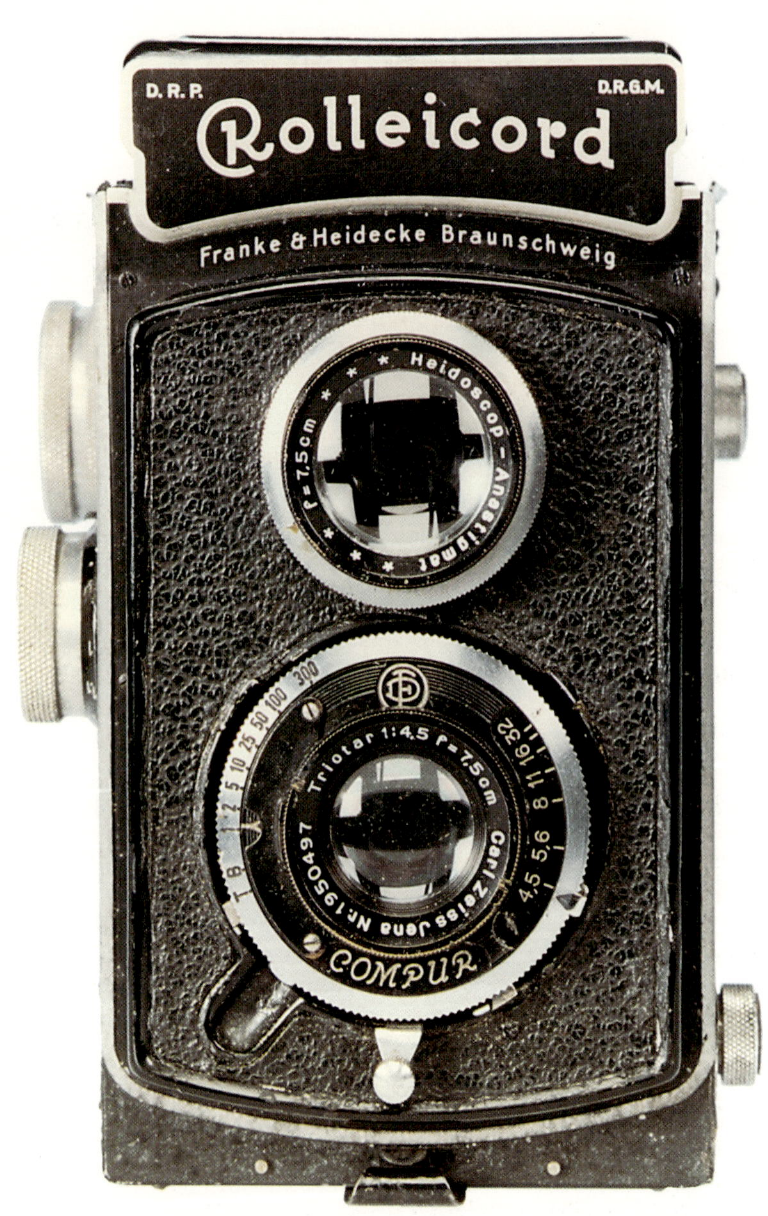

1937 Rolleicord Ia Type 4.5
No. 5RC 530

Rolleicord Ia Type 4.5

Factory Model
5RC 530 Model 1a Type 4.5

Launch Date
00-05-1937

Factory Termination Date
03-01-1938

Serial Numbers
1,945,000 -2,183,000
On Taking Lens

Taking Lens
Carl Zeiss Triotar
f4.5/75mm

Finder Lens
Heidoscop-Anastigmat
f4/75mm

Shutter
Deckel Compur Rim Set

Speeds
T, B, 1, 1/2, 1/5, 1/10,
1/25, 1/50, 1/100, 1/300

Filter Size
28.5mm Push-on

Film Size
120 or 35mm with Rolleikin

Dimensions
13.4 x 9.4 x 9.6cm

Weight
738g (26oz)

Launch Price Germany RM96 USA $65 UK £18.75

Identification
f4.5 taking lens, internal film counter, hood sports finder. "Franke & Heidecke Braunschweig" name in small type below the Rolleicord name. No F&H logo on hood. Model 520 F&H logo on hood, no sports finder.

Variations
No variations reported, except for the exposure guide which is in different languages. The focusing distance scale is calibrated in metres. This camera is often confused with model 520, the main difference being the sports finder, and lens number.

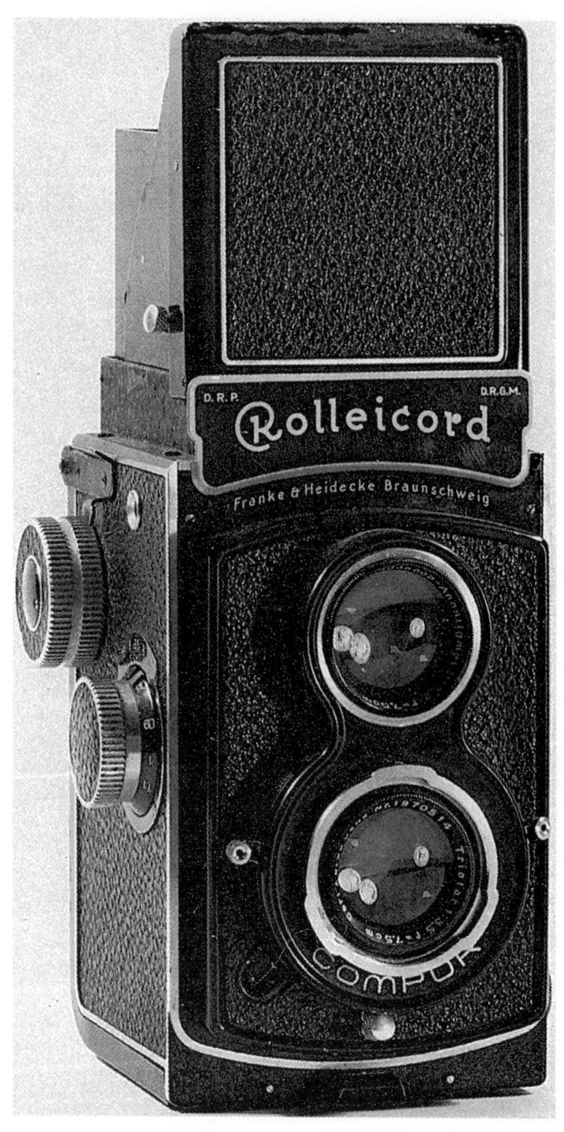

1937 Rolleicord IIa F3.5
No. 5RC 540
Photo courtesy of Rollei - Museum camera on loan to Universal Film Studios, USA

Rolleicord IIa F3.5

Factory Model
5RC 540 Model IIa

Launch Date
15-06-1937

Factory Termination Date
20-01-1938

Serial Numbers
1,966,000 - 2,124,000
On Taking Lens

Taking Lens
Carl Zeiss Triotar
f3.5/75mm

Finder Lens
Heidoscop-Anastigmat
f3.2/75mm

Shutter
Deckel Compur

Speeds
B, T, 1, 1/2, 1/5, 1/10, 1/25
1/50, 1/100, 1/300

Filter Size
28.5 Push-on/Bayonet 1

Film Size
120 or 35mm with Rolleikin

Dimensions
9.7 x 13.5 x 9.3cm

Weight
782g (27½oz)

Launch Price German RM128 USA $65 UK £16.50

Identification
The only Rolleicord with etched nameplate and bayonet mount on taking lens. Problems occurred with close up accessories requiring push-on 28.5mm for finding lens and Bayonet 1 on taking lens.

Variations
When supplies of the cast nameplate with camera identification number were delivered this model continued in production as Model No.541.

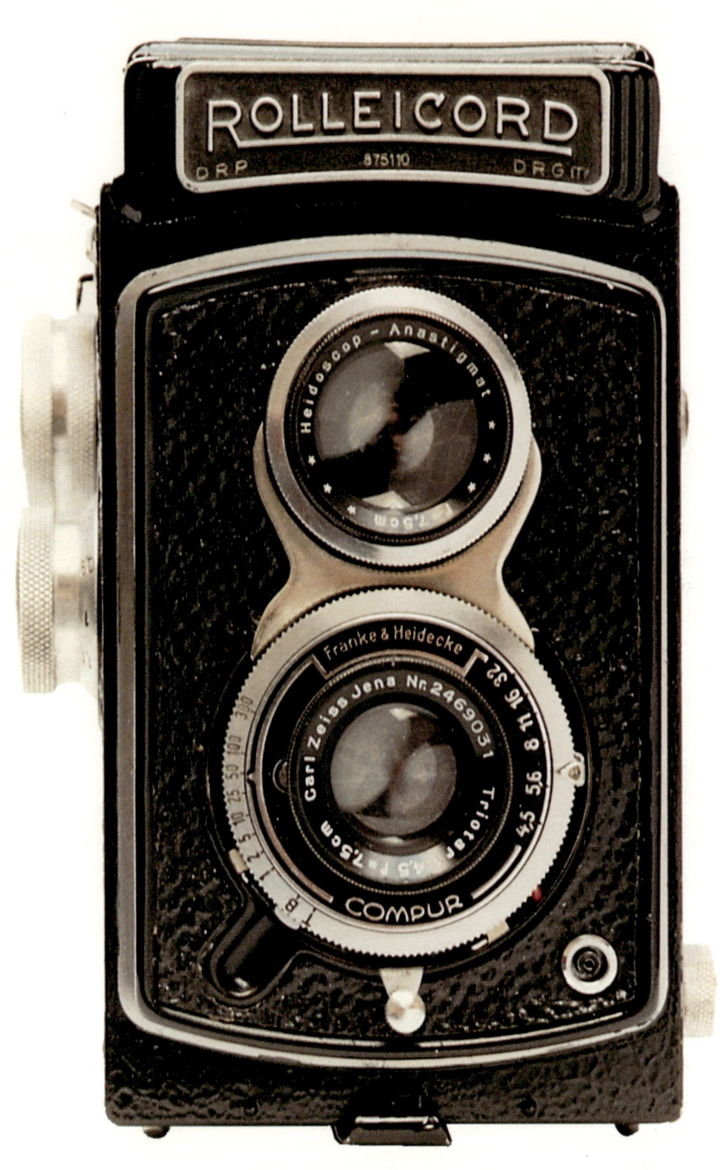

1938 Rolleicord
No. 5RC 531 Model Ia/III
with f4.5 lens

Rolleicord Ia Type 3

Factory Model
5RC 531 Model 1a/III

Launch Date
02-02-1938

Factory Termination Date
1945

Serial Number
611,000 - 1,042,999
Located on cast nameplate

Taking Lens
Carl Zeiss Triotar
f4.5/75mm

Finder Lens
Heidoscop-Anastigmat
f4/75mm

Shutter
Deckel Compur Rim set

Speeds
T, B, 1, 1/2, 1/5, 1/10,
1/25, 1/50, 1/100, 1/300

Filter Size
28.5mm Push-on

Film Size
120 or 35mm with Rolleikin

Dimensions
10 x 9.5 x 13.5cm

Weight
814g (28¾oz)

Launch Price Germany RM128 USA $55 UK £14.50

Identification

This was the only Rolleicord with a cast nameplate and f4.5 taking lens, and to have the "Franke and Heidecke" name on the shutter above the taking lens. The first Rolleicord to use chromium plate that replaced nickel plating. This model used existing stocks of the rim set shutter and f4.5 lens. Note Model No.531 dates from 1936 - it was delayed through late deliveries of the cast nameplates.

Variations

Exposure guide on back in various languages. If the focusing knob was calibrated in metres then the markings were black on silver and if they were calibrated in feet then the markings were white on black. Metal plate between the lenses. Serial numbers were taken from Model Nos. 541, 542 and 543 until all old f4.5 lenses were sold.

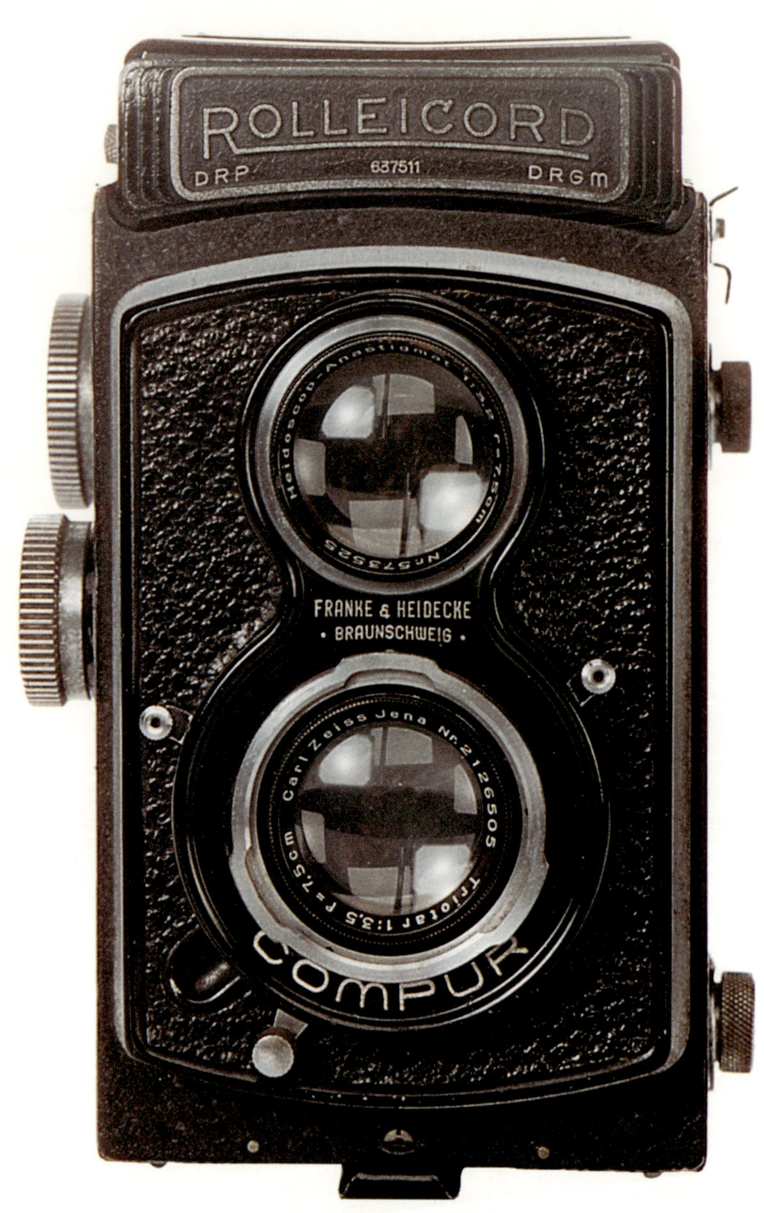

1938 Rolleicord
No. 5RC 541 Model IIb

Rolleicord IIb

Factory Model
5RC 541 Model IIb

Launch Date
00-02-1938

Factory Termination Date
00-01-1939

Serial Numbers
612,000 - 858,999
Located on nameplate

Taking Lens
Carl Zeiss Triotar
f3.5/75mm

Finder Lens
Heidoscop-Anastigmat
f3.2/75mm

Shutter
Deckel Compur

Speeds
T, B, 1, 1/2, 1/5, 1/10, 1/25, 1/50, 1/100, 1/300

Filter Size
Bayonet 1 on Taking Lens
28.5mm on Finder Lens

Film Size
120 or 35mm with Rolleikin

Dimensions
13.8 x 9.1 x 9.4cm

Weight
760g

Launch Price Germany RM128 USA $65 UK £15.75

Identification
Similar to model number 540 except for cast nameplate and no sports finder in hood. Taking lens only with Bayonet I for attaching filters and accessories. "Franke and Heidecke, Braunschweig" name between lenses, "Compur" in large letters at the bottom of the taking lens. No sports finder.

Variations
Exposure guide on back, this was available in different languages, including Chinese. See Model No.531, page 39, for f4.5 lens with the above serial numbers.

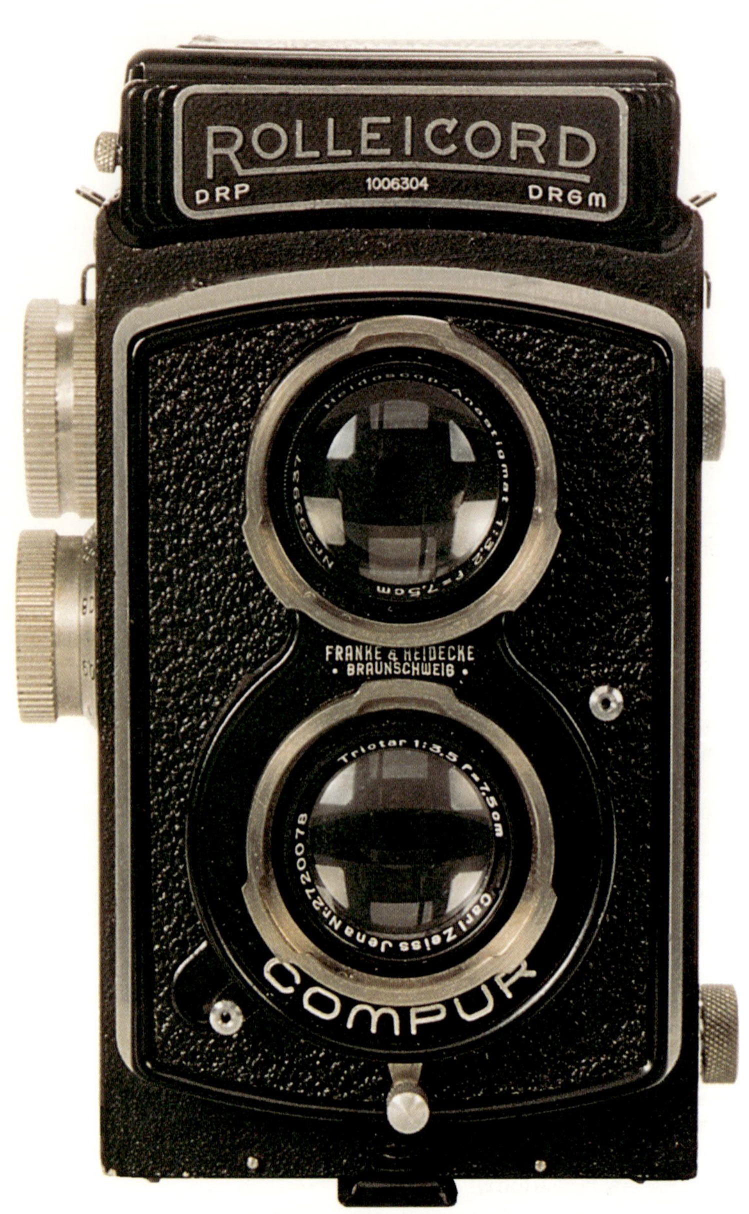

1939 Rolleicord
No. K3 542 Model IIc

Rolleicord IIc

Factory Model
K3 542 Model IIc

Launch Date
00-09-1939

Factory Termination Date
00-07-1949

Serial Numbers
859,000 - 1,006,999

Taking Lens
Carl Zeiss Triotar
f3.5/75mm

Finder Lens
Heidoscop-Anastigmat
f3.2/75mm

Shutter
Deckel Compur

Speeds
T, B, 1, 1/2, 1/5, 1/10,
1/25, 1/50, 1/100, 1/300

Filter Size
Bayonet 1

Film Size
120 or 35mm with Rolleikin

Dimensions
9.4 x 13.5 x 9.6cm

Weight
850g (30oz)

Launch Price Germany RM128 USA $90 UK £16.50

Identification
Only Rolleicord with top shutter speed 1/300th and Bayonet I on both taking and finding lens. No sports finder. Note "Compur" in large letters under taking lens.

Variations
Some sources give termination number 980,000 or 999,999 in 1949. Alec Pearlman author of the original 1953 Rollei TLR manual was given the last camera with a compur 1/300 shutter by Paul Franke shortly before he died; the camera number, 1,006,304, is in the Jersey Photographic museum. Due to a shortage of parts during the war, some cameras' finder lenses are without name plates and are nickel plated instead of chrome. The numbers are around 998,000 - 999,999. The exposure scales on the camera back are in different languages. See Model No.531, page 39, for f4.5 lens with the above serial numbers.

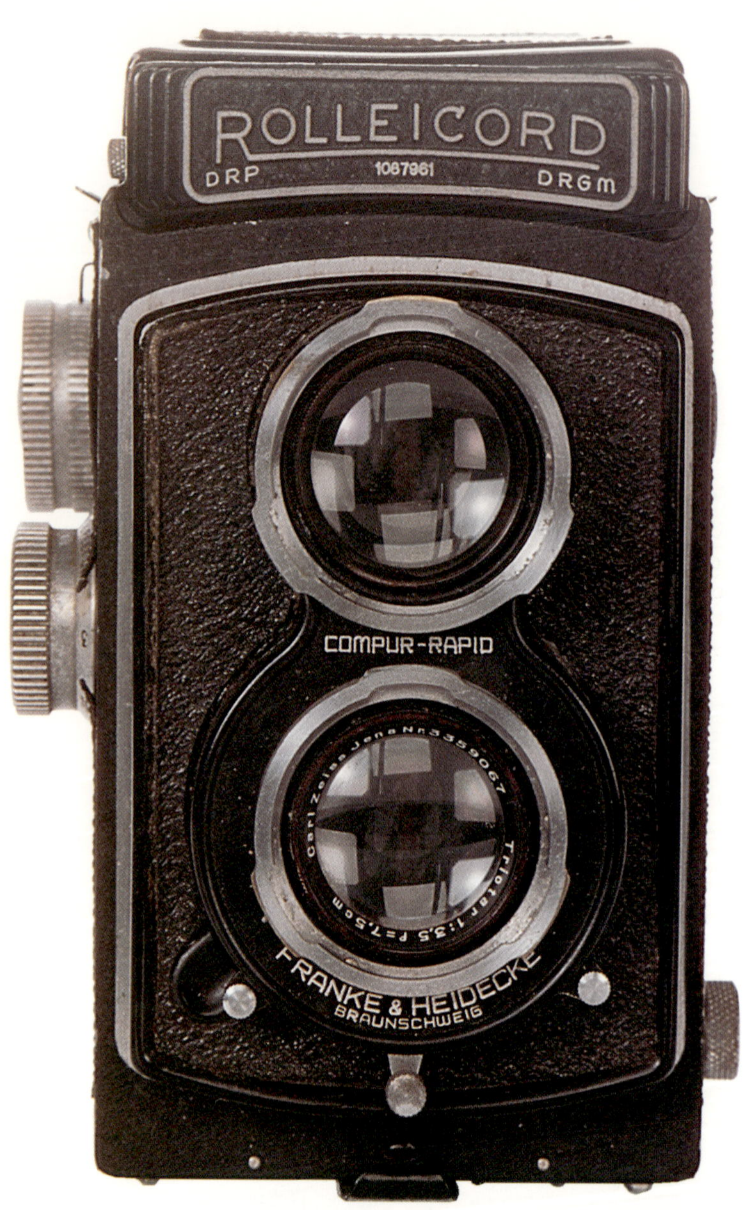

1949 Rolleicord
No. K3 543 Model IId

Rolleicord IId

Factory Model
K3 543 Model IId

Launch Date
00-11-1949

Factory Termination Date
31-10-1950

Serial Numbers
1,007,000 - 1,134,999

Taking Lens
Carl Zeiss Triotar
f3.5/75mm

Finder Lens
Heidoscop-Anastigmat
f3.2/75mm

Shutter
Deckel
Compur-Rapid

Speeds
B, 1, 1/2, 1/5, 1/10, 1/25, 1/50, 1/100, 1/250, 1/500

Filter Size
Bayonet 1

Film Size
120 or 35mm with Rolleikin

Dimensions
9.4 x 13.5 x 9.6cm

Weight
850g (30oz)

Launch Price Germany RM220 USA $157 UK £68.30

Identification

"Compur-Rapid" name between lens; " Franke & Heidecke Braunschweig" under taking lens. There is a red window in the base. Shutter speed 1/500th. Bayonet 1 fitting on both lenses, critical focusing at eye level.

Variations

Usual camera back with film exposure tables in different languages with focusing now calibrated in metres or feet. The finder lens is found without a nameplate, and the "Compur Rapid" and "Franke and Heidecke" names can be found in two different type styles. For Xenar lens model see Model No.544, page 47. See Model No.531, page 39, for f4.5 lens with the above serial numbers.

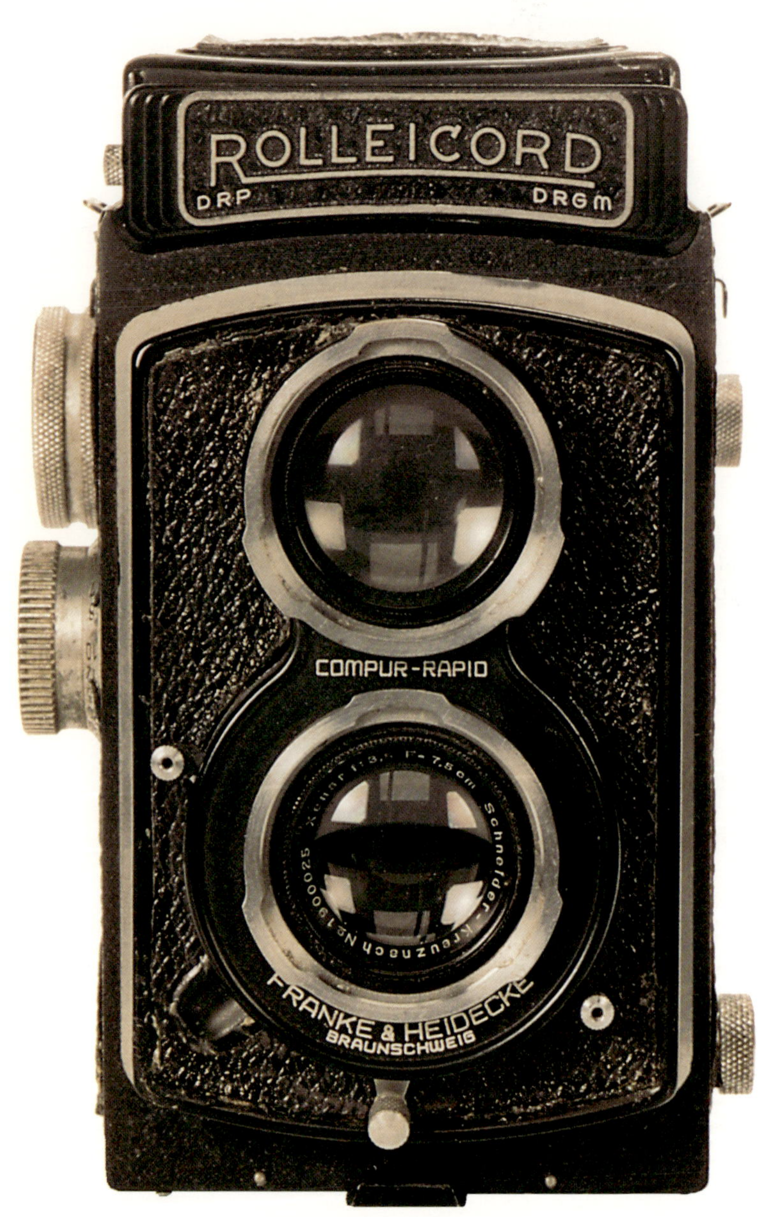

1949 Rolleicord
No. K3 544 Model IIe Xenar Lens

Rolleicord IIe Xenar Lens

Factory Model
K3 544 Model IIe

Launch Date
01-07-1949

Factory Termination Date
31-10-1950

Serial Numbers
1,135,000 - 1,135,999

Taking Lens
Schneider Xenar
f3.5/75mm

Finder Lens
Heidosmat
f3.2/75mm

Shutter
Deckel`
Compur-Rapid

Speeds
B, 1, 1/2, 1/5, 1/10, 1/25,
1/50, 1/100, 1/250, 1/500

Filter Size
Bayonet 1

Film Size
120 or 35mm with Rolleikin

Dimensions
9.4 x 13.5 x 9.6cm

Weight
850g (30oz)

Launch Price Germany RM238 USA $140 UK £69

Identification
Same as model 543 except for Schneider Xenar lens. The start date was given as 20-09-1949 but the Xenar lens option appears in the Rollei April 1949 German price list.

Variations
For Carl Zeiss Triotar lens version see Model No.543, Type 5. Note speeds to 1/500th possible with Compur Rapid shutter.

Special Note
For Rolleicord with f4.5/75mm Xenar lens see page 65, Special Rolleicord Models.

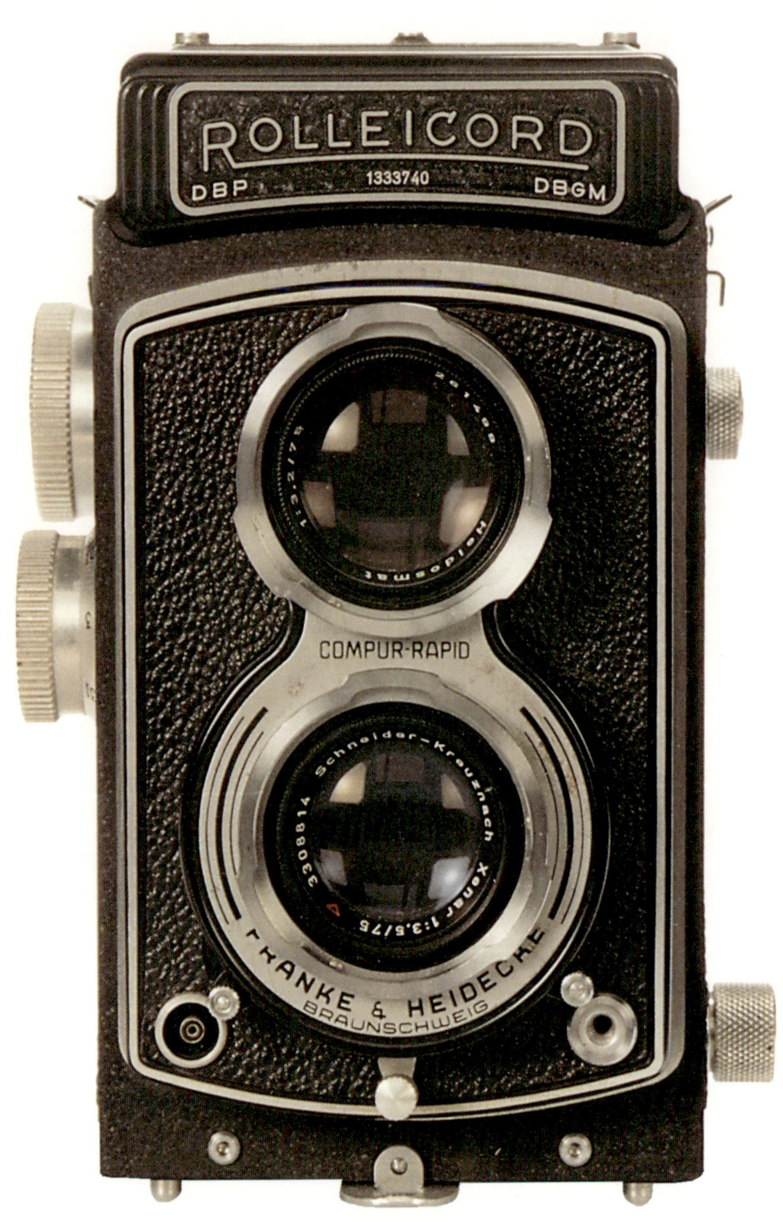

1950 Rolleicord
No. K3 B Model III

Rolleicord III

Factory Model
K3 B Model III

Launch Date
26-09-1950

Factory Termination Date
03-07-1953

Serial Numbers
1,137,000 - 1,344,050

Taking Lens
Zeiss Opton Triotar or
Schneider Xenar f3.5/75mm

Finder Lens
Heidosmat
f3.2/75mm

Shutter
Deckel Compur-Rapid

Speeds
B, 1, 1/2, 1/5, 1/25, 1/50,
1/100, 1/250, 1/500

Filter Size
Bayonet 1

Film Size
120 or 35mm with Rolleikin

Dimensions
14 x 9.3 x 9.5cm

Weight
830g (29 1/3rd oz)

Launch Price Germany RM298 USA $130 UK £69.15

Identification

No red window for positioning film. When loading film into camera, film is positioned with arrows pointing at 2 red marks. Factory fitted X Synchronization. Film wind on knob with 17mm centre - previous model 542/3 with 13mm centre. New designed hood with three studs and Rollei logo.

Variations

From camera number 1,157,000 an adjustable film pressure plate allows Rolleikin 2 35mm adapter to be fitted without replacing the camera back. The Schneider Xenar lens cost approx. $10, DM20, £5 more than the West German Zeiss Opton 3 element Triotar.

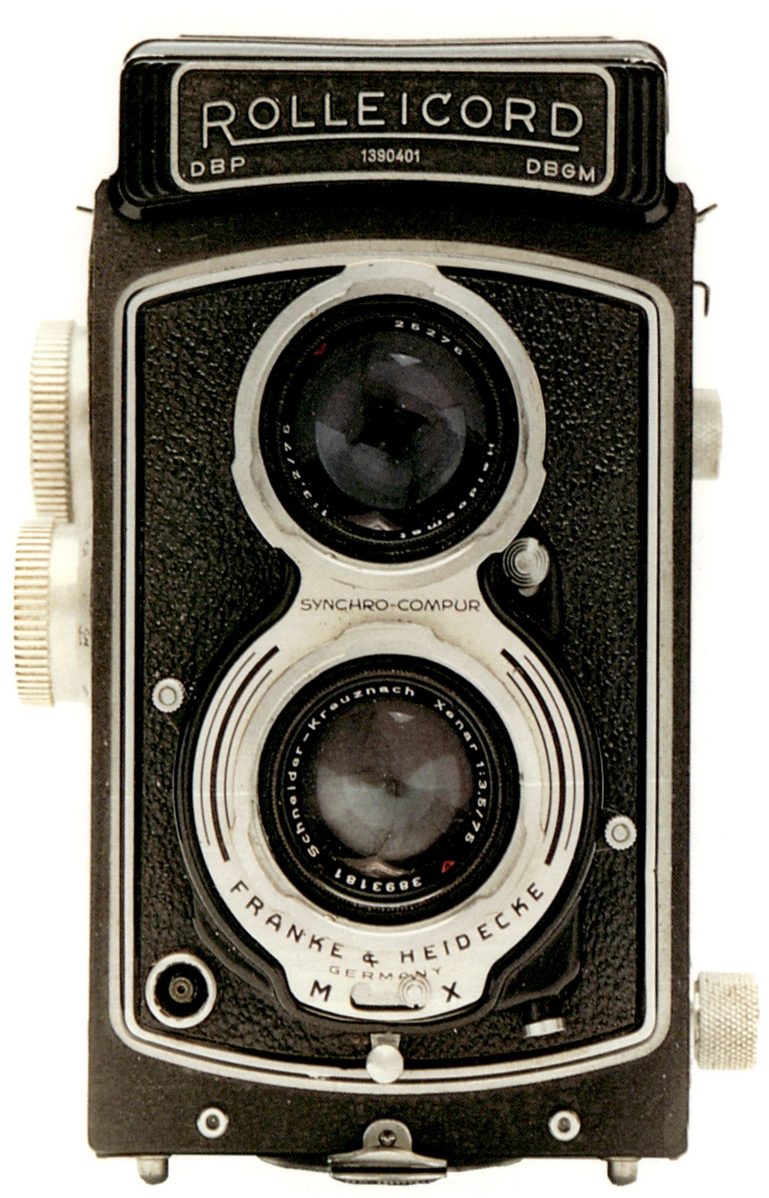

1952 Rolleicord
No. K3C Model IV

Rolleicord IV

Factory Model
K3C Model IV

Launch Date
07-04-1952

Factory Termination
20-10-1954

Serial Numbers
1,344,051 - 1,390,999

Taking Lens
Schneider Xenar
f3.5/75mm

Finder Lens
Heidosmat
f3.2/75mm

Shutter Deckel
Synchro-Compur

Speeds
B, 1, 1/2, 1/5, 1/25, 1/50,
1/100, 1/250, 1/500

Filter Size
Bayonet 1

Film Size
120 or 35mm with Rolleikin

Dimensions
14 x 9.7 x 10cm

Weight
845g (30oz)

Launch Price Germany DM338 USA $149 UK £69.15

Identification

MX Synchronization located below taking lens. Synchro-Compur shutter name between lens. Switch for multiple exposures. Small focusing knob not popular hence short production run. Note MX switch below taking lens. In future models this switch was located on adjoining side of finder lens.

Variations

Although the three element Triotar lens was advertised in American price lists no cameras were so fitted or appeared in the German dealers' price lists for 1952, '53 or '54. Some sources give the start date as 1953 when the camera first appeared in the USA due to overstocking of Cord III.

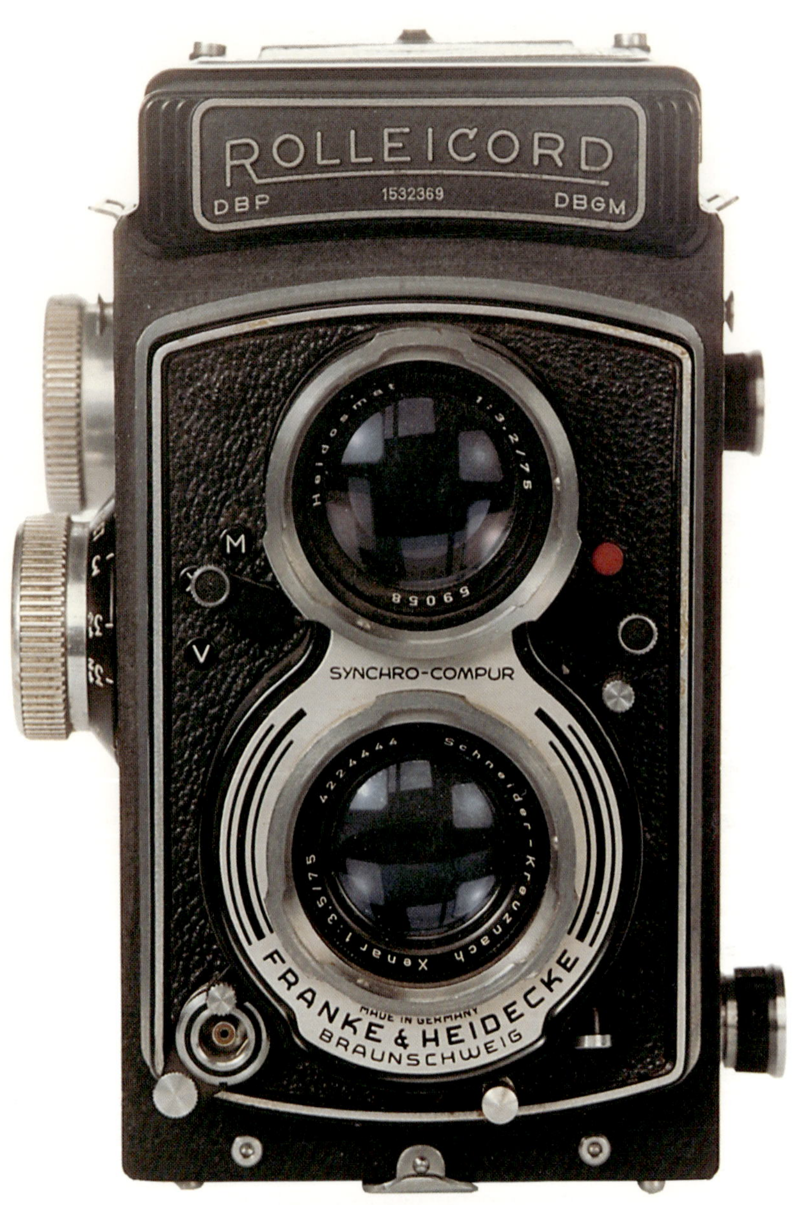

1954 Rolleicord
No. K3D Model V

Rolleicord V

Factory Model
K3D Model V

Launch Date
18-10-1954

Factory Termination Date
28-02-1957

Serial Numbers
1,500,000 - 1,583,999

Taking Lens
Schneider-Xenar
f3.5/75mm

Finder Lens
Heidosmat
f3.2/75mm

Shutter
Deckel
Synchro-Compur MXV

Speeds
B, 1, 1/2, 1/4, 1/8, 1/15, 1/30, 1/60, 1/125, 1/250, 1/500

Filter Size
Bayonet 1

Film Size
120 or 35mm with Rolleikin

Dimensions
14 x 9.8 x 10cm

Weight
915g (32oz)

Launch Price Germany DM338 USA $134.55 UK £58.45

Identification

MXV Synchronization. New large focusing knob 28mm on right-hand side (when using camera), later models on the left-hand side. Exposure guide on back now in picture form to suit all languages.

Variations

The Jersey Photographic Museum has seen many versions of the Rolleicord V. The finder and taking lens numbers do not fall into any pattern. The Rolleicord V Xenar lens, as on previous model, has the red Schneider triangle kite mark. This was discontinued from about camera number 1,535,000.

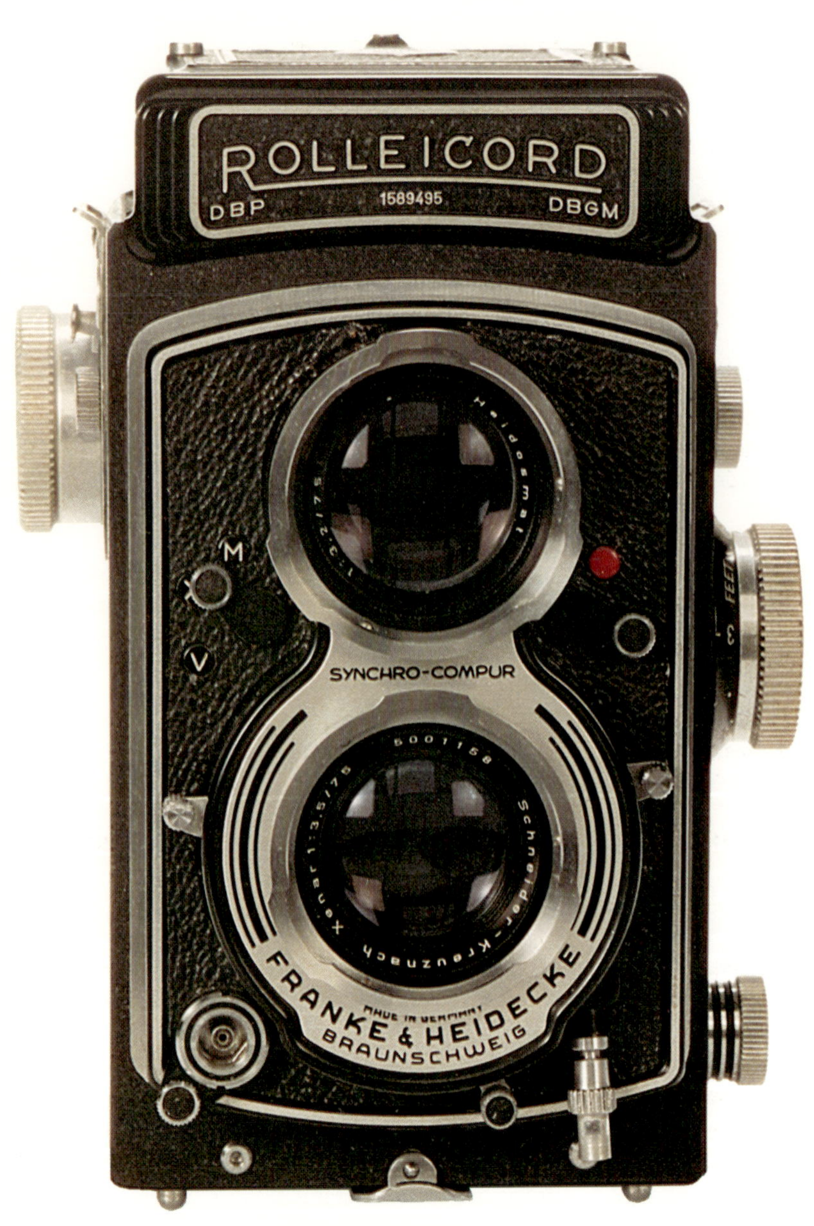

1957 Rolleicord
No. K3E Model Va

Rolleicord Va Type 1

Factory Model
K3E Model Va

Launch Date
29-04-1957

Factory Termination Date
00-06-1958

Serial Numbers
1,584,000 - 1,599,999

Taking Lens
Schneider Xenar
f3.5/75mm

Finder Lens
Heidosmat
f3.2/75mm

Shutter
Deckel
Synchro-Compur MXV

Speeds
B, 1, 1/2, 1/4, 1/8, 1/15, 1/30, 1/60, 1/125, 1/250, 1/500

Filter Size
Bayonet 1

Film Size
120 or 35mm with Rolleikin

Dimensions
14.2 x 9.7 x 9.8cm

Weight
881g (31oz)

Launch Price Germany DM338 USA $124.50 UK £58.50

Identification

Focusing knob now on left-hand side whereas all previous models on the right-hand side; this allowed a new interchangeable film counter for different formats. With this provision the Rolleicord Va warranted a different model No.

Variations

Should your EV scale (for setting camera speed and exposure to your EV meter reading) be on the left side, your camera is a Rolleicord Va Type 1; the right side, for model Va type 2.

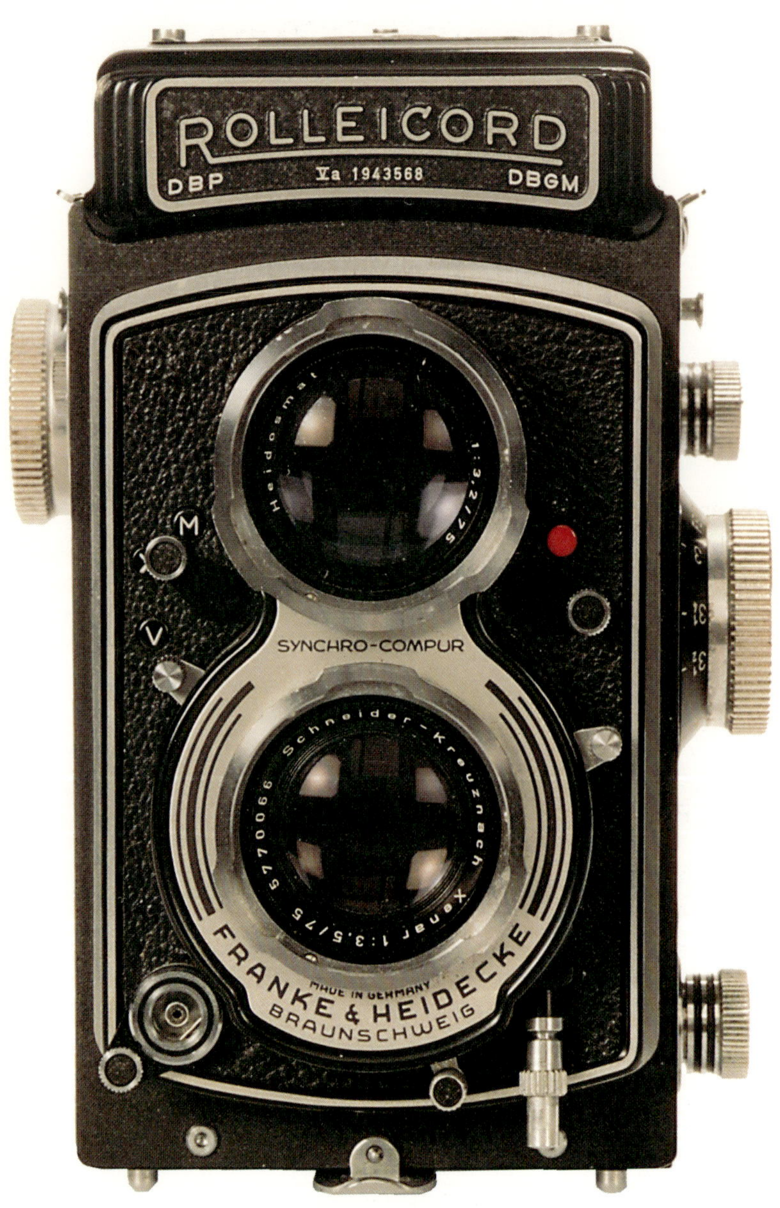

1958 Rolleicord
No. K3Ea Model Va Type 2

Rolleicord Va Type 2

Factory Model
K3Ea Model Va

Launch Date
00-06-1958

Factory Termination Date
18-01-1961

Serial Numbers
1,900,000 - 1,943,999

Taking Lens
Schneider Xenar
f3.5/75mm

Finder Lens
Heidosmat
f3.2/75mm

Shutter
Deckel
Synchro-Compur MXV

Speeds
B, 1, 1/2, 1/4, 1/8, 1/15, 1/30,
1/60, 1/125, 1/250, 1/500

Filter Size
Bayonet 1

Film Size
120 or 35mm with Rolleikin

Dimensions
14.2 x 9.7 x 9.8cm

Weight
881g (31oz)

Launch Price Germany DM338 USA $99.50 UK £59.50

Identification
Identical to Va Type I except EV scales now on right-hand side of taking lens. Finder lens un-numbered.

Variations
Last batch numbered 1,943,000-1,943,999 preceded by Va on cast nameplate. Chrome Sync. connection instead of normal black circle. All the examples seen have distance calibration marked in feet, nevertheless the local domestic model was calibrated in metres.

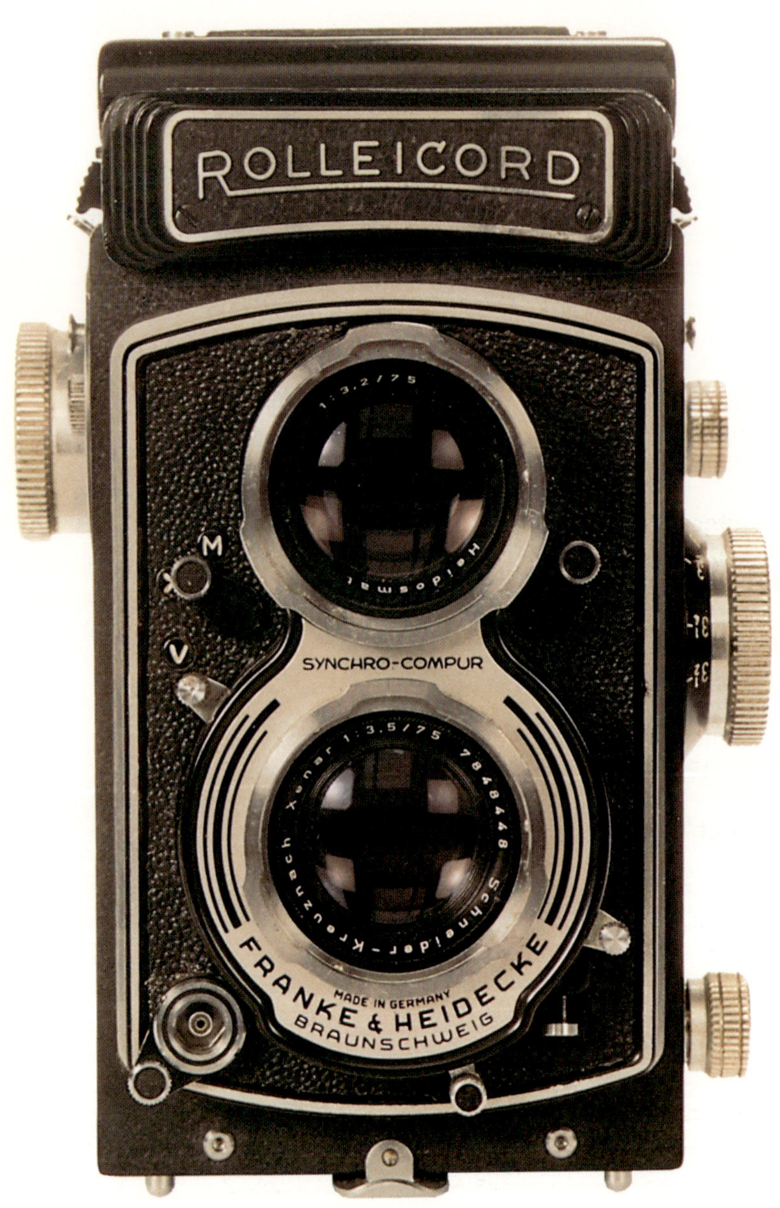

1962 Rolleicord
No. K3F Model Vb

Rolleicord Vb Type 1

Factory Model
K3F Model Vb

Launch Date
08-03-1962

Factory Termination Date
03-02-1970

Serial Numbers
2,600,000 - 2,649,999

Taking Lens
Schneider Xenar
f3.5/75mm

Finder Lens
Heidosmat
f3.2/75mm

Shutter
Deckel
Synchro-Compur MXV

Speeds
B, 1, 1/2, 1/4, 1/8, 1/15, 1/30,
1/60, 1/125, 1/250, 1/500

Filter Size
Bayonet 1

Film Size
120 or 35mm with Rolleikin

Dimensions
14.2 x 10 x 10cm

Weight
940g (33¼oz)

Launch Price Germany DM360 USA $99.50 UK £62

Identification

The letters "Vb" precede the camera serial number above nameplate. Removable hood allows the use of a prism. "Franke & Heidecke" name under taking lens, and incorporated MX Synchronization that was omitted from types 2 and 3.

Variations

There are three variations of the Vb Rolleicord, Type 1 with "Franke & Heidecke" name under taking lens, Type 2 with "Rollei-Werke", and Type 3 with "Rollei-Werke Franke & Heidecke". Grey leathered cameras provided for Philips' Oscillograph - see page 65.

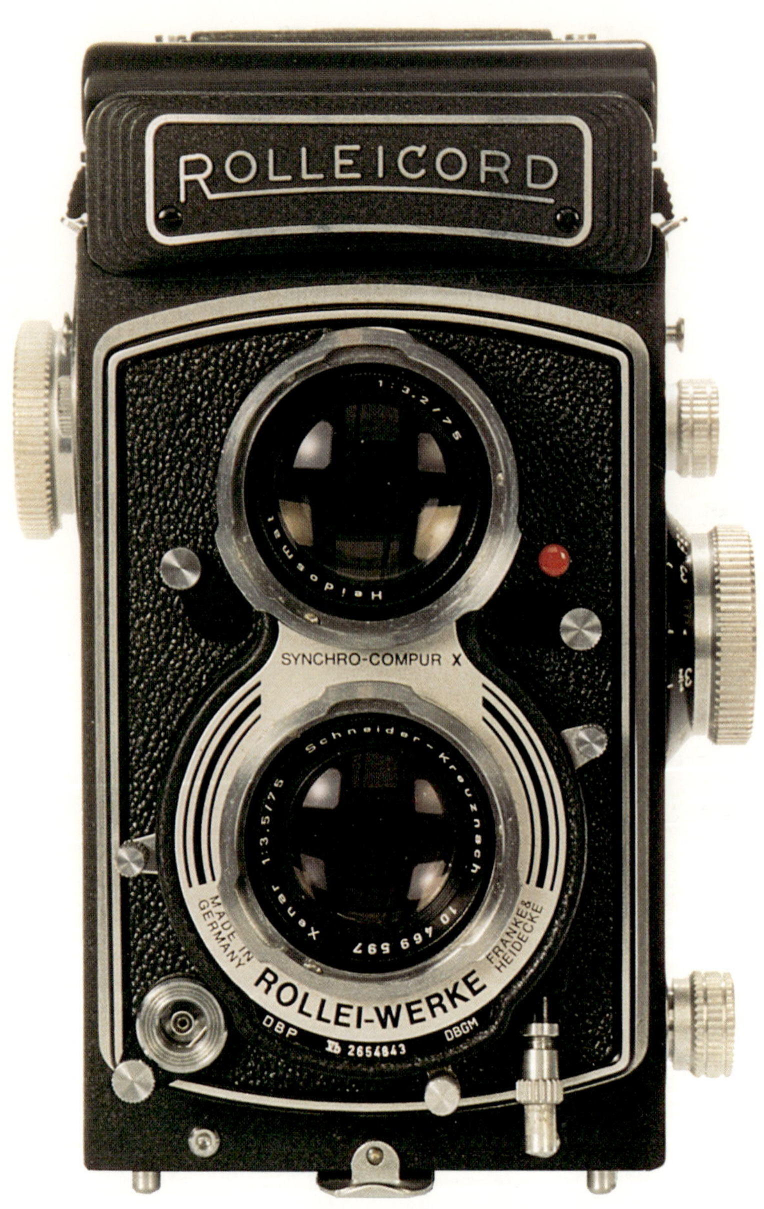

1970 Rolleicord
No. K3Fa Model Vb Type 2

Rolleicord Vb Type 2

Factory Model
K3Fa Model Vb

Launch Date
03-02-1970

Factory Termination Date
00-06-1971

Serial Numbers
2,650,000 - about 2,665,999

Taking Lens
Schneider Xenar
f3.5/75mm

Finder Lens
Heidosmat
f3.2/75mm

Shutter
Deckel
Synchro-Compur X

Speed
B, 1, 1/2, 1/4, 1/8, 1/15, 1/30, 1/60, 1/125, 1/250, 1/500

Filter Size
Bayonet 1

Film Size
120 or 35mm with Rolleikin

Dimensions
14.2 x 10 x 10cm

Weight
940g (33¼oz)

Launch Price Germany DM350 USA $199.50 UK £89.50

Identification

"Rollei-Werke" name below taking lens with camera serial number located below, preceded by the letters "Vb". No, you have not got a pre-production or un-numbered prototype, if you were looking for the number on the hood! X only Synchronization and marked between the lens "Synchro-Compur X".

Variations

Two types of logo can be seen on the hood: the thin Rollei scroll was phased out in mid 1970 for a bolder typeface. Many Cord Vb's and most of the last Rolleiflex T's were sold to the British Ministry of Defence; hoods could easily be interchanged. A few cameras were constructed with grey leather for the Middle East market. Focusing scale calibrated in metres or feet.

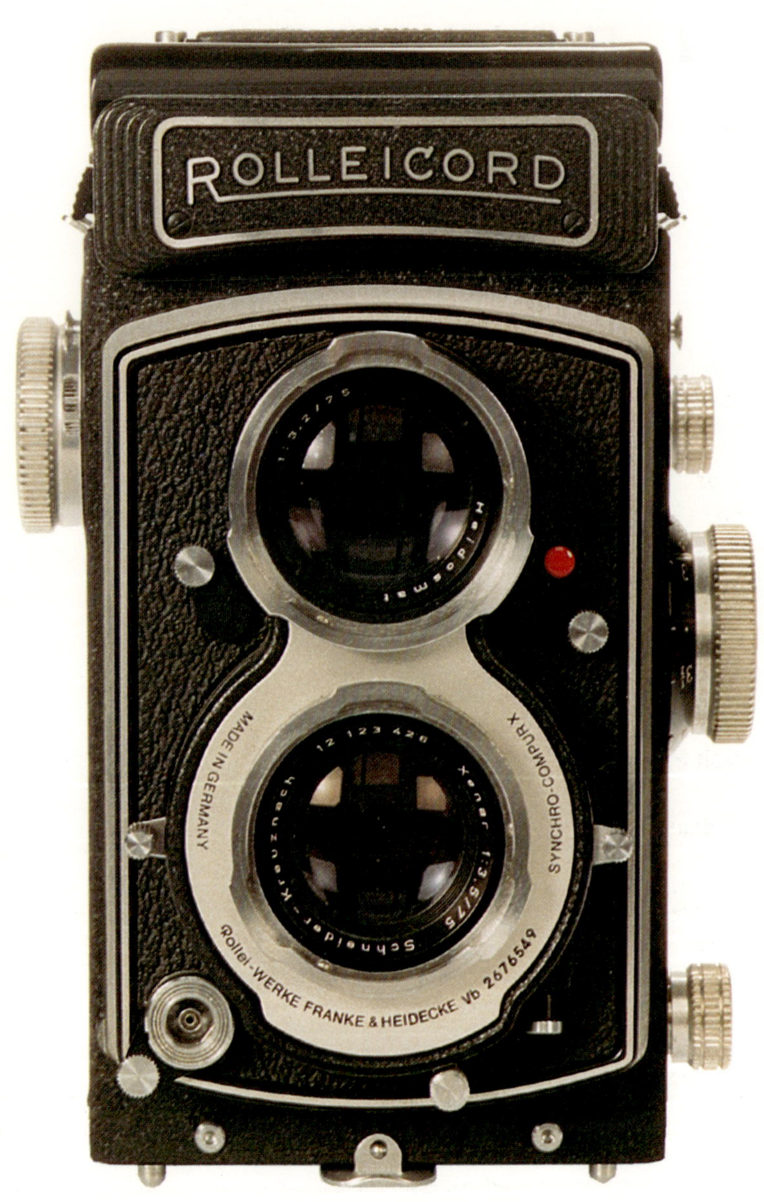

1971 Rolleicord
No. K3Fb Model Vb Type 3

Rolleicord Vb Type 3

Factory Model
K3 Fb Model Vb

Launch Date
00-06-1971

Factory Termination Date
00-03-1976

Serial Numbers
About 2,666,000 - 2,677,498

Taking Lens
Schneider-Xenar
f3.5/75mm

Finder Lens
Heidosmat
f3.2/75mm

Shutter
Deckel
Synchro-Compur XV

Speeds
B, 1, 1/2, 1/4, 1/8, 1/15, 1/30, 1/60, 1/125, 1/250, 1/500

Filter Size
Bayonet 1

Film Size
120 or 35mm with Rolleikin

Dimensions
14.2 x 10 x 10cm

Weight
940g (33¼oz)

Launch Price Germany DM368.52 USA $219.50 UK £99

Identification

New front lens panel was introduced, which was nick-named "White Face" with the new company name of "Rollei-Werke Franke & Heidecke" below the letters "Vb" and the camera serial number. Only 11,498 Type 3 were constructed. There was a new type of black leather. It was the same as the 1971 Rolleiflex, also the nameplate was held in place by two sunken black screws rather than protruding chrome and black screws.

Variations

No Rolleicord Vb's were constructed with a Tessar lens for sale. Five cameras for sampling with Tessar lens were submitted to the British Ministry of Defence who were the largest single customer for the Rolleicord Vb and Rolleiflex T. This entire production was covered in black leather. This is a very usable camera and mint condition examples can be found and bought for the same price as a zoom compact. Note that in 1976, with tax, the UK price was £134.59.

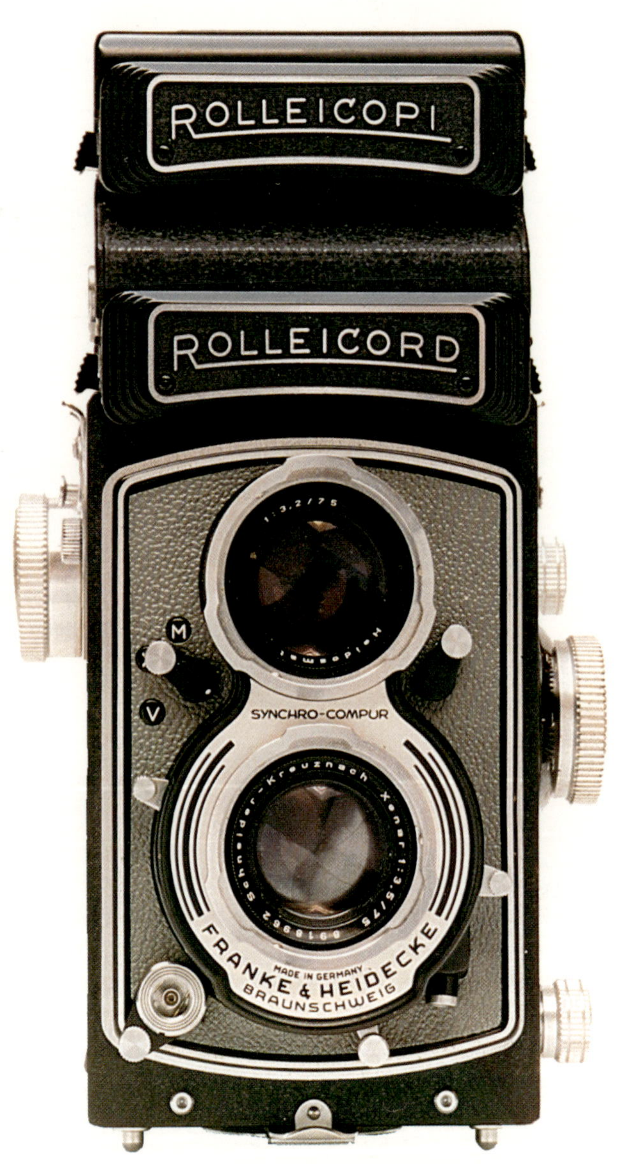

1962/8 Rolleicord
No. Philips K3Vba
Note grey colour

Special Rolleicord Models

Rolleicord cameras were available, "Made to special order", and were not sold to the general public. In time these cameras will come into the second-hand market, and no doubt will be sought after by collectors. The publishers would welcome any information not listed within this manual, especially serial numbers that differ from those here published. Please note many cameras have been cannibalised with one part used on another or a new part fitted without serial number. To ensure omissions or inaccuracies are corrected in future editions please write to Club Rollei, Jersey Photographic Museum, Hotel de France, St. Saviour's Road, St. Helier, Jersey, Channel Islands, JE2 7LA.

SPECIAL ROLLEICORDS

Date	Serial Numbers	Quantity	Model	Remarks
1939	999,500-999,999	500	**532**	Unusual Carl Zeiss f4.5Tessar supplied to German Police. Lens shutter panel similar to Art Deco Cord.
1947/48	Unknown	1000	**K3542a**	With Schneider f4.5/ 75mm Xenar. Information from Irwin Smoler, USA, confirmed by Rollei.
1962 1968	2,610,000-2,610,999 2,632,000-2,632,999	1000 1000	**K3 Vba**	This Grey Rolleicord ordered for Philips Oscillograph recording. Information supplied by Derek Ward & Claus Prochnow
1962	2,611,000-2,611,499	500	**K3 Vbb**	Grey Rolleicords supplied to German Police.
1962	87,500-87,599	100	**5RC 531**	Believed special camera with flash Sync. socket for microscope work.

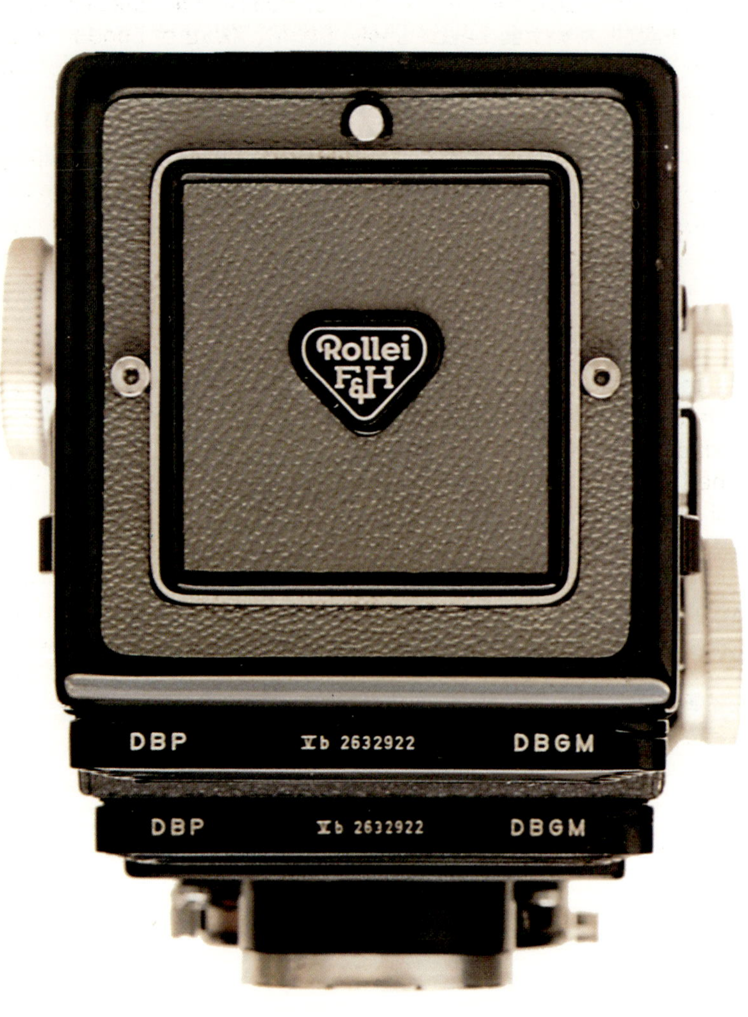

Philips Oscillograph Grey Rolleicord Vb

ADDITIONAL OBSERVATIONS

The Philips Oscillograph recording device No.PM9300 was part of a complete system sold only by Philips to scientific and technical establishments. Information has been supplied by D. Ward of London and C. Prochnow of Braunschweig. Rollei club members have also provided some interesting insights to this Rolleicord.

The outfit was supplied in a small fitted attaché case containing a grey standard Rolleicord Vb, and having a Polaroid back with the same serial number as the camera using Type 32, 37 or 38 5.6 x 8cm Polaroid film. Also supplied were a Rolleicopi focusing unit, to place between the camera's screen and hood, a pair of special Rolleinar 4 close up lenses (focusing range 25-20cm), together with special lens hoods.

Other features included a set of 16 and 32 frame counters, to replace the standard 12; masks for 4 x 5.5 and 2.8 x 5.5 images; and an attachment for fixing the camera over the Oscillograph screen. All major items were finished in grey, including the attaché case that also carried the camera's serial number.

We were told that the official Rollei numbers were 2,610,000 to 2,610,350. However, it would appear that numbers allocated terminated at 2,610,999. Mr. Ward's own camera number is 2,610,008, whereas three cameras at the Jersey Photographic Museum have the numbers 2,610,451, 2,610,529 and 2,632,922. Club members' own cameras are in the 26104xx, 26105xx and 26106xx range.

It is likely that other special orders were placed for the Rolleicord. Should you have any information please inform the publishers.

Pre-War Rolleiflex

Serial Nos.	Model No.	Factory No.	Year	Page No.
1 - 199,999	Original 6x6	K1 611/612	1928	71
200,000 - 567,000	Standard	6RF 620	1932	73
		6RF 621	1932	73
200,000 - 567,550	Standard	6RF 622	1934	75
568,516 - 805,000	Automat 1	6RF 111A	1937	77

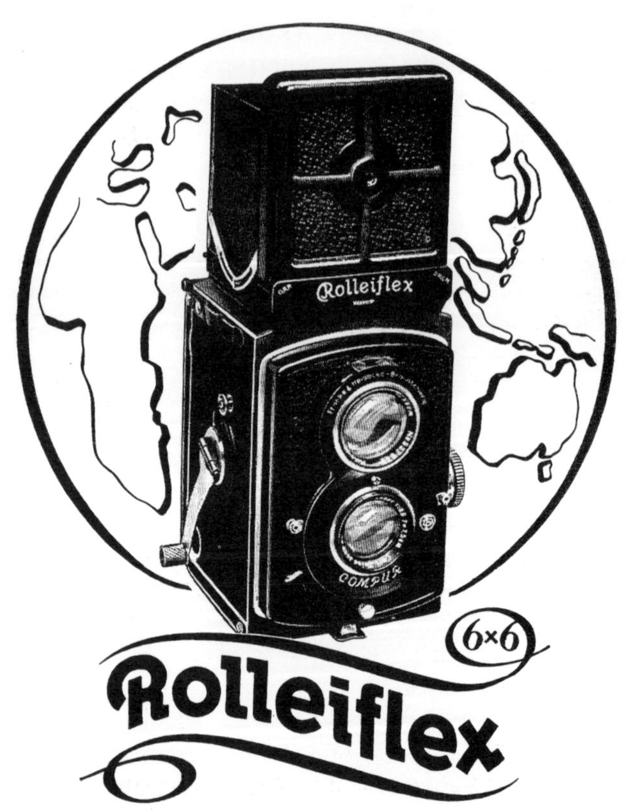

Pre-War Rolleiflex

Although the idea of the original Rollei TLR was born in 1916 it was not until 1926 that Reinhold Heidecke started in earnest to design his dream camera. In 1927 the first prototype was constructed and in the following year a further ten. By 1928 the final design was decided upon. Twelve production sample cameras were made, and the camera went on sale after the provisional patent was granted on the 17th January 1929. Although missing the important pre Christmas period for sales, 3,881 cameras had been sold in the first two years. During this period all Rollei cameras, including the stereo Heidoscop and Rolleidoscop were constructed in the cellars and first floor of a private house at 31/32 Viewegstraße. In 1932 Franke and Heidecke moved into their new, modern spacious factory and from then on, the Rolleiflex camera was greatly improved and refined.

Many ask how the name "Rolleiflex" came about. The name was derived: "Roll" from Rollfilm, "ei" the second and third letters from Reinhold or Heidecke, and "Flex" from reflex. The name Rolleiflex is still used on today's 2.8GX TLR manufactured by Rollei.

From the collector's point of view the pre-war Rolleiflex TLR cameras are interesting, as progress in manufacturing during this period can be easily traced. From the basic sheet metal which was cut, bent and joined to the later power press stamped forms. The basic cast frame has withstood 60 years with little change from the original.

German Patents, Trademarks, Etc.:

DRP	Deutsches Reichs Patent
DBP	Deutsches Bundes Patent
DRGM	Deutsches Reichs Gebrauchs Musterschutz (Trademark)
DBGM	Deutsches Bundes Gebrauchs Musterschutz (Trademark)
V	Vorlaufwerk (Self-timer)
X	Synchronization Electronic Strobe Flash
MX	M Exposures of 1/50 to 1/500 with Flash Lamps

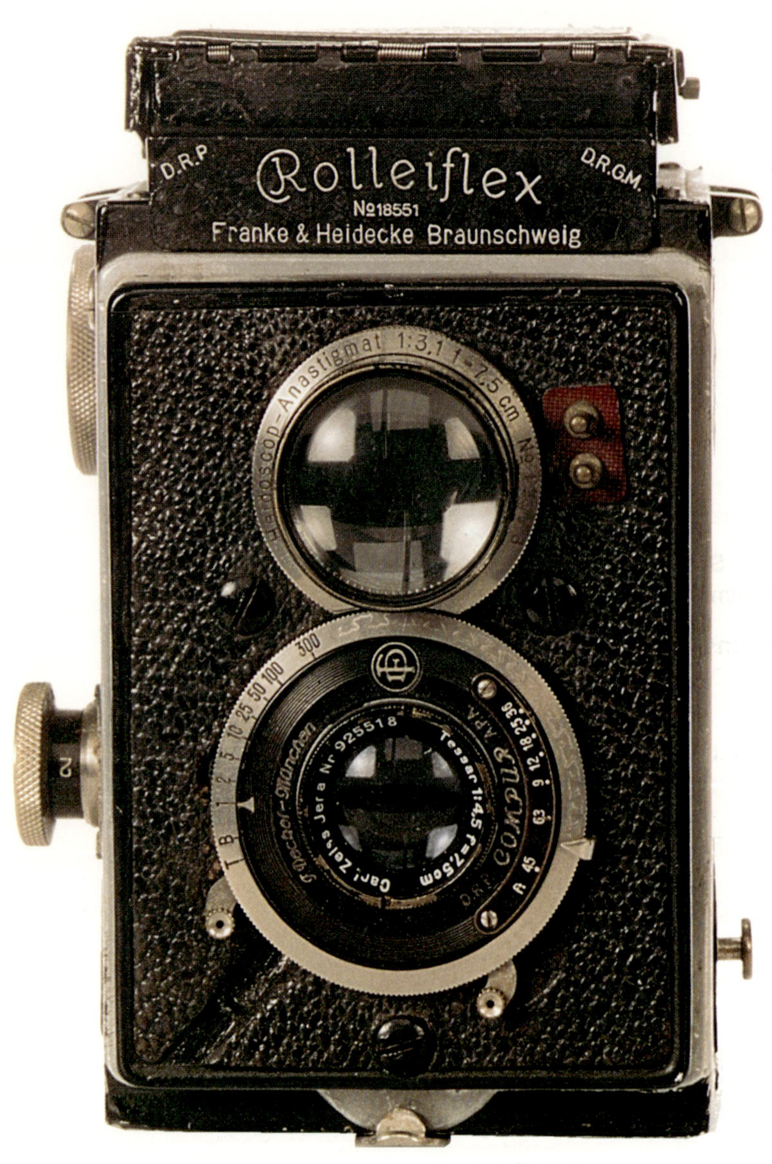

1930 Original Rolleiflex
_No. K1 611/612_
with non factory installed synchronization

Original Rolleiflex 6x6

Factory Model
K1 611/612

Launch Date
December 1928

Factory Termination Date
February 1932

Serial numbers
1 - 199,999

Taking Lens
Zeiss Tessar f4.5/75mm
Zeiss Tessar f3.8/75mm

Finder Lens
Heidoscop
f3.1/75mm

Shutter
F.Deckel-Compur

Speeds
1/300, B, T

Filter Size
28.5mm Push-on

Film Size
B.1. (117)

Dimensions
13 x 8.3 x 9.6cm

Weight
f4.5 lens = 715g,
f3.8 lens = 722g

Launch Price (611/612)			
Germany	RM198/225	USA	$75.00/$85.00
UK	£16.35/ £18.75		

Identification

This original Rolleiflex with film advance winding knob had no lever wind, and the back was not hinged, whereas in later models the back was hinged, with a film lever wind. This simplifies identification of the original Rolleiflex.

Variations

Many owners converted the Original camera to accept 620 or 120 films. The camera was not fitted with an internal film counter but a firm in Berlin provided a kit. As sales of this first Rollei TLR increased, Franke & Heidecke were able to afford additional machinery resulting in improved design. Many improvements could be found on later models of the original i.e. hinged back, polished film pressure plate, instead of the black original painted version, and focus knob with distance calibration, etc.. Original strap guides were made from cast metal. They were later made out of formed brass.

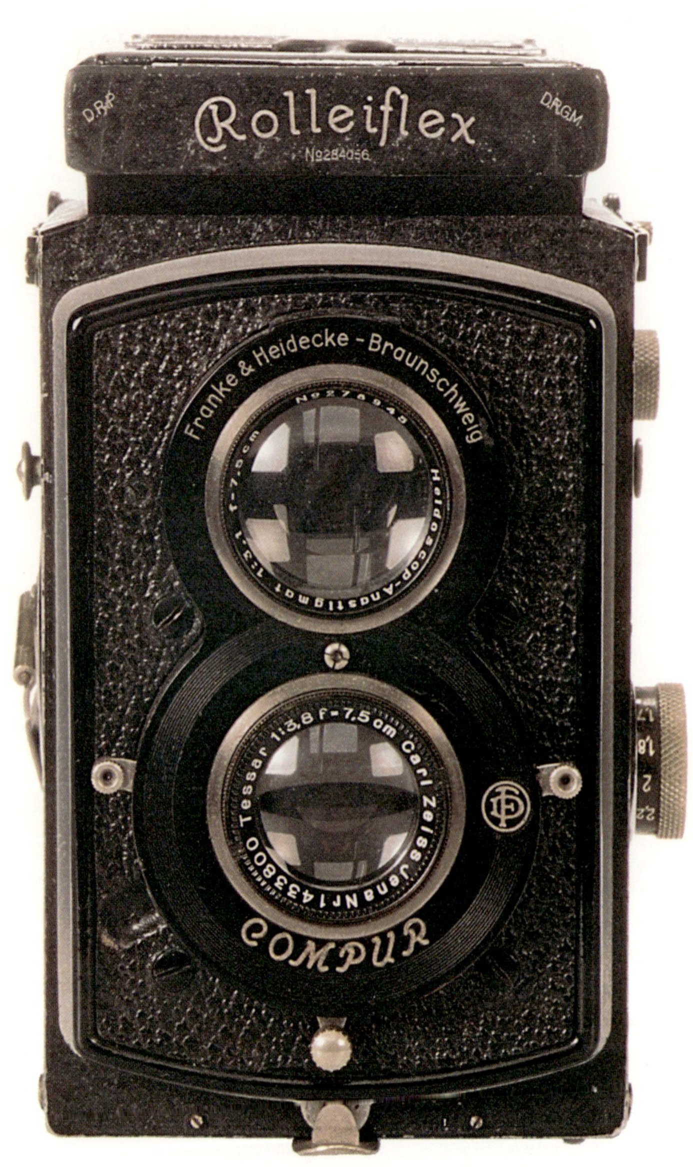

1932 Standard Rolleiflex
No. 6RF 621
with f3.8 lens

Original Standard Rolleiflex Model 620/621

Factory Model
Standard 6x6 6RF 620,
6RF 621

Launch Date
Jan 1932 (620)
Feb 1932 (621)

Factory Termination Date
May 1938 (620)
Jan 1935 (621)

Serial Numbers
200,000 - 567,000

Taking Lens
Model 620 f4.5/75mm Tessar
Model 621 f3.8/75mm Tessar

Finder Lens
Heidoscop
f3.1/75mm

Shutter
F.Deckel Synchro-Compur
Rim Set

Speeds
1/300, B, T

Filter Size
28.5 Push-on

Film Size
120

Dimensions
14.3 x 8.6 x 9cm

Weight
773g (620)
803g (621)

Launch Price	Germany	RM198/220	USA	$125/$138.00
	France	FF1750/2000	UK	£17.50/£19.00

Identification
Lever film wind, hinged back. Metal etched nameplate filled with white paint. "Compur" name below taking lens. The original and the original standard were the only Rolleiflexes to have either f4.5 or f3.8 lenses.

Variations
Accessories included 35mm Rolleikin adapter to accept 35mm film, plate back adapter, and 2 close up push on Proxars size 24mm on Finder lens, and 28.5mm on Taking lens.

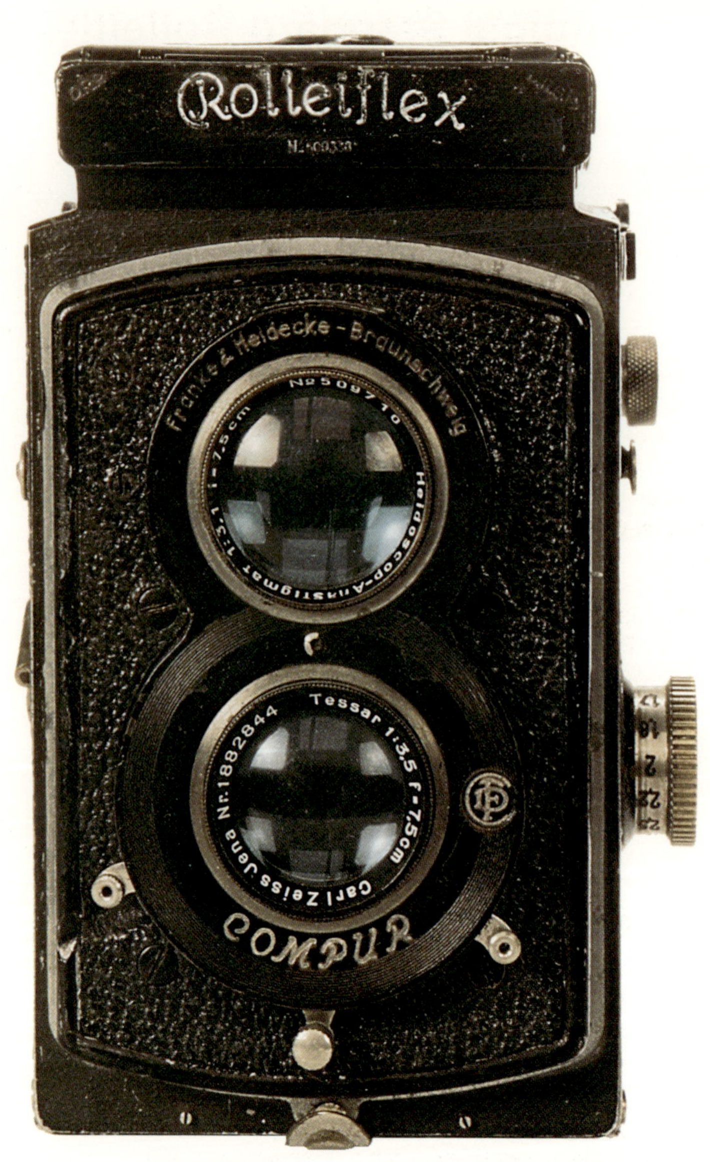

1936 Standard Rolleiflex
No. 6RF 622
with f3.5 lens

Standard Rolleiflex Model 622

Factory Model
Standard 6x6 6RF 622

Launch Date
November 1934

Factory Termination Date
May 1938

Serial Numbers
200,000 - 567,550

Finder Lens
Zeiss Tessar
f3.5/75mm

Taking Lens
Heidoscop-Anastigmat
f3.5/75mm

Shutter
F.Deckel-Compur
Rapid

Speeds
1/300, B, T

Filter Size
28.5mm Push on

Film Size
120

Dimensions
14.3 x 8.6 x 9cm

Weight
778g

Launch Price Germany RM242 | France FF1800 | USA $112.00 | UK £18.00

Identification

This is the only f3.5 Rolleiflex without a Bayonet on the taking lens. The numbers were also used on the original standard f4.5 and f3.8 lens versions. Popular for panoramic landscape photography, a bubble level was incorporated on the viewing screen. The exposure guide is on the back.

Variations

The exposure guide is in different languages on the camera back. On checking cameras in the Jersey Photographic Museum it was found that on the English exposure guide 2 numbers were incorrect and this was changed on later models. Until 1936 edging on backs painted black and thereafter chrome plated, with two decorative screws diagonally opposite screws for back hinge.

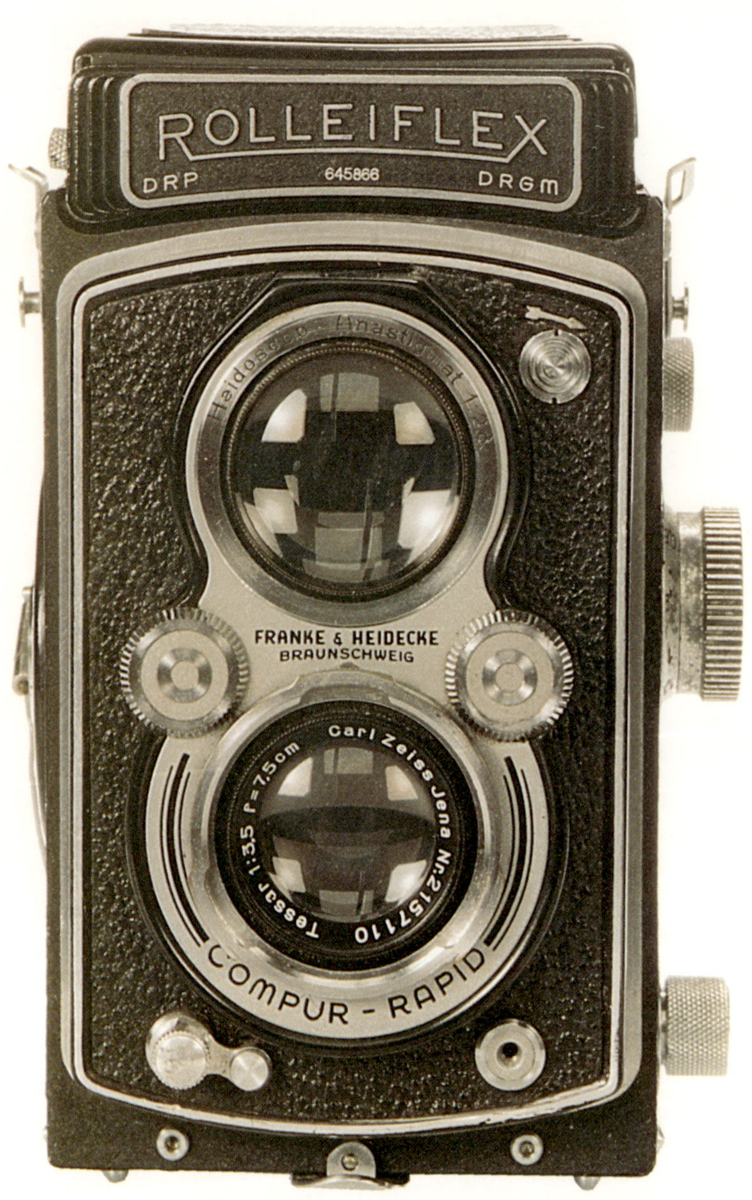

1937 Rolleiflex Automat
No. RF 111A Model 1

Automat 6x6 Model 1

Factory Date
Automat 6x6 RF 111A

Launch Date
Feb. 1937

Factory Termination Date
Jan. 1939

Serial Numbers
568,516 - 805,000

Taking Lens
Carl Zeiss Jena Tessar
f3.5/75mm

Finder Lens
Heidoscop
f2.8/75mm

Shutter
F.Deckel Synchro-Compur
Rapid

Speeds
1/500, B

Filter Size
Bayonet 1

Film Size
120 or 35mm with Rolleikin

Dimensions
14.3 x 8.6 x 9cm

Weight
850g

Launch Price Germany RM240 USA $130.00 UK £19.95

Identification
This is the only Rolleiflex with double Bayonets on the taking lens, while the finder lens accepts 28.5mm push on filter. There is no red window, cranking the wind on lever automatically cocks the shutter. On the top right-hand corner, there is a built-in delayed timer for a period of 10 secs. Aperture and speeds are adjusted by 2 wheels with grey centres above the taking lens, whereas past camera wheels had black centres.

Variations
There is a safety lock for shutter release on later models. The exposure guide on the camera back is in different languages.

Rollei 9 X 9 Studio Camera

Much has been written about this camera, in fact eleven pages in the 'History of Rollei', also by Ian Parker (the author of this book), were devoted to this subject. 14 cameras were constructed although only two appear to have survived, both of which are in the Braunschweig Städtisches Museum, to whom we are indebted for the photograph showing the studio camera together with some interesting Rollei prototypes. The Studio Camera is the big fish, there are 12 unaccounted for. It is known that one could be in Canada and another in the USA. The author would like to hear of the whereabouts of a Rollei 9 x 9 Studio Camera, whether dead or alive!

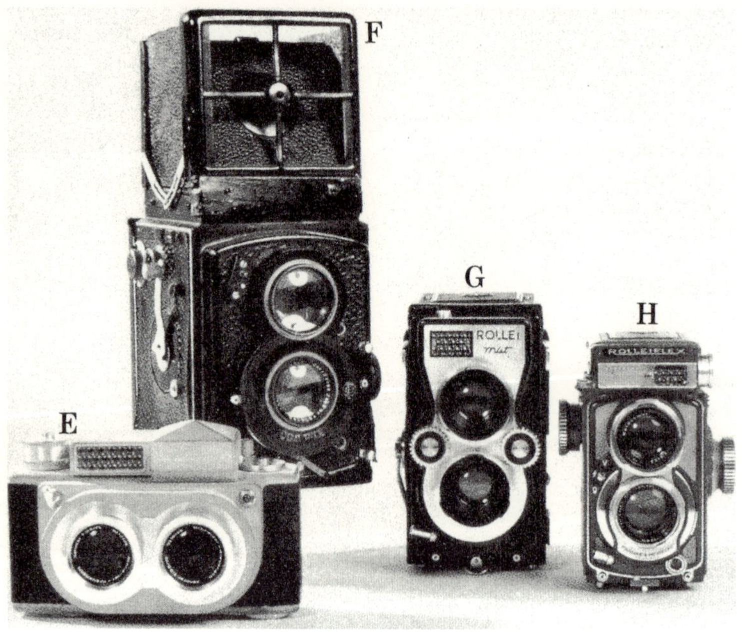

Prototypes:

E - 1954 35mm Stereo
F - 1933 9x9 Studio TLR
G 1959 Rollei Magic
H - 1959 Baby 4x4 with meter

Studio Camera:

Factory Model	No. 9RF 122	**Date**	1933
		Serial Numbers	unknown
Taking Lens	100mm f4.5 Tessar	**Finder Lens**	100mm Heidosmat
Dimensions	18 x 11.5 x 13 cm	**Film size**	122 Rollfilm

Post-War Rolleiflex 3.5f

We have cheated in this section by including the 1939 automat and new standard Rolleiflexes. These cameras were the first Rolleiflexes with Bayonet I fittings to both finder and taking lenses. These models are similar to the post-war 1945 models, so, to avoid confusion and incorrect identification, all 3.5 Rolleiflexes with Bayonet fittings on both lenses will be found in this section.

Franke and Heidecke were fortunate in that war damage to their factory was minimal, and the British 21st army group, who took over control of the factory, did, through various ways and by obtaining replacement machine tools, enable production to re-commence. Thus in the immediate post-war years, the factory prospered. It was not until 1949 that the first true new post-war design went on sale known as the Automat K4 model 50, which some have named the X, as this was the first model with X Synchronization as a standard feature.

Almost each year the model saw some modification and it is for this reason we have included the launch date year into the particular model's name. The breakthrough to the 3.5F Rolleiflex came with the introduction of the factory installed exposure meter in 1956 on the 3.5E and it is this model, together with the later 3.5F that most users prefer today, with second-hand prices constantly increasing.

The Rolleiflex "T" a budget priced Rolleiflex is today in great demand by wedding photographers, costing a third less than the 3.5F second-hand. The largest single order coming from the UK Ministry of Defence and used extensively by the British Army and Royal Navy. So popular was the Rollei TLR with the British army that Rollei had to restart their production line in late 1971 when they received an order for 5000 Rollei T's to be taken over the next 5 years, with the last camera completed on the 12th May 1976.

The name "T" most people assume means "T" for Tessar as Rollei 3.5 cameras at that time were fitted with Zeiss Planar or Schneider Xenotar lenses. In fact Rolleicord cameras as well as the 1955-56 Automat Rolleiflex had Tessar lenses. The T model was partly designed by Theodore Uhl, a university graduate, who designed the plastic parts in the

Rolleicord Va, well hidden from prying eyes. With the resultant saving in cost the elderly Reinhold Heidecke asked Uhl and his young team to design an economic budget priced 3.5 Flex. So that costs could be separated from the new 3.5F also being designed at this time all orders for the Uhl design were signed Theodore and his department was know as T. The management did not realise that the T did not refer to Tessar and, when they ultimately found out, Theodore reminded them that as Heidecke had used part of his name in the "Rolleiflex" name, he should be allowed to do the same. The management did not agree and he was promptly dismissed.

The most desired post war Rolleiflex is the 220 model whereby 24 or 12 exposures can be achieved by adjusting a small lever and, of course, by using the 220 size film for 24 exposures. This camera today commands a high price and is much sought after.

What the difference is between the Zeiss Planar and the Schneider Xenotar lens is another question often asked. The answer is nothing. Tests between similar cameras with either the Xenotar or Planar lens have shown identical results. The pre 1965 Zeiss f3.5 Planar had 5 elements and a sixth tinted optical element was added to the rear of the lens to act as a UV/Skylight filter to remove the blue cast found on many colour slides at that time. For monochrome this made no difference but many have wrongly assumed that any pre 1965 f3.5 Planar lens was no good - far from it. As the chief designer of Carl Zeiss said at the time "some people judge the quality of a photographic lens by the number of its elements. This is not a reliable criterion at all. The number of elements is determined by technical specifications such as aperture, angle of view, and, in addition, the dimensions for fitting are different for each type of camera. Some lenses, for example the famous four element Zeiss Tessar, prove that it is not the number of elements that counts, it is the image quality that is the guiding feature in the construction of Zeiss Lenses."

Many collectors have a 5 element f3.5 Planar Rolleiflex as well as the 6 element 1965 f3.5 starting with number 2,800,000. The prototype f3.5 fitted with 6 elements was No.2,753,000 manufactured in September 1964. The sixth element was a cheaper option than coating the front element lens at that time.

Post-War Rolleiflex

Serial Nos.	Model No.	Factory No.	Year	Page No.
805,000 - 1,050,000	Automat 2	K4 B	1939	83
805,000 - 927,999	New Standard	K4-640	1939	85
1,050,000 - 1,099,999	Automat 3	K4 B2	1945	87
1,000,000 - 1,168,000	Automat 'X'	K4 Mod.50	1949	89
1,200,000 - 1,427,999	Automat 4	K4 A	1951	91
1,428,001 - 1,479,999	3.5 MX-EVS	K4 B	1954	93
1,479,000 - 1,739,999	3.5 MX-EVS	K4 B	1954	93
1,740,000 - 1,787,849	3.5 E	K4 C	1956	95
1,850,000 - 1,868,442	3.5 E	K4 C	1956	95
1,870,000 - 1,872,010	3.5 E2	K4 C2	1959	97
2,480,000 - 2,482,999	3.5 E2	K4 C3	1960	97
2,380,000 - 2,385,034	3.5 E3	K4 C3	1961	99
2,100,000 - 2,199,999	T 1	K8 T	1958	101
2,220,000 - 2,313,999	T 2	K8 T2	1966	103
2,314,000 - 2,320,298	T 3	K8 T3	1971	105
2,200,000 - 2,219,999	3.5 F1	K4 D	1958	107
2,230,000 - 2,241,500	3.5 F2	K4 E	1960	109
2,250,000 - 2,299,999	3.5 F3	K4 F	1960	111
2,800,000 - 2,844,999	3.5 F4	K4 F/1	1965	113
2,845,000 - 2,857,149	3.5 F5	K4 F/2	1979	115
3,555,000 - 3,559,999	3.5 F5	K4 F/2	1979	115

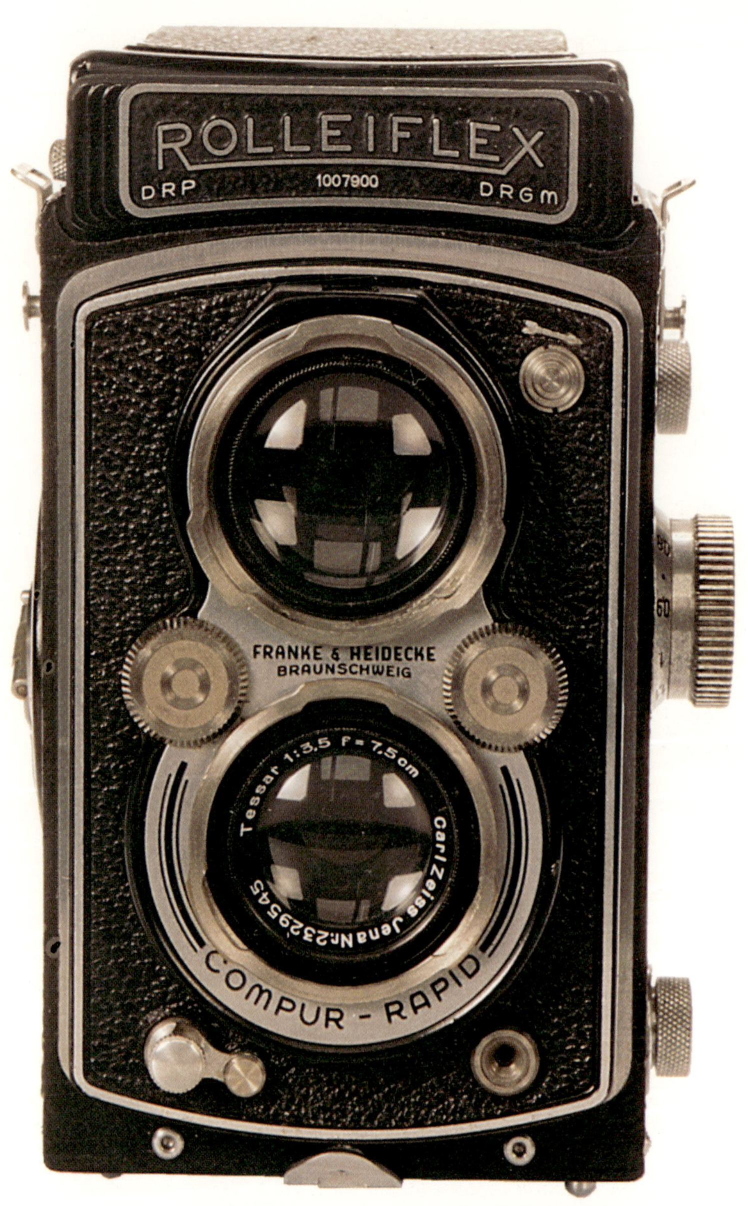

1939 Automat Rolleiflex
No. 6x6 K4B Model 2

Automat Rolleiflex Model 2

Factory Model
Automat 6x6 K4 B

Launch Date
01-02-1939

Factory Termination Date
11-10-1945

Serial Numbers
805,000 - 1,050,000

Taking Lens
Carl Zeiss Jena Tessar
f3.5/75mm

Finder Lens
Heidoscop-Anastigmat
f2.8/75mm

Shutter
F.Deckel Compur
Rapid

Speeds
1 - 1/500, B

Filter Size
Bayonet 1

Film Size
120 or 35mm with Rolleikin

Dimensions
14 x 9 x 9.5cm

Weight
928g

Launch Price

Germany	RM240	USA	$145.00
UK	£31.25		

Identification

N.B. The same serial numbers were allotted to both the Automat model 2 and the New Standard cameras. Shutter and aperture control wheels with grey coloured inserts, double Bayonet I on both lenses. The Compur - Rapid logo is located under the taking lens.

Variations

Flash Synchronization socket was available as an option from the factory and it was located in the centre below the taking lens. Examples with sync. sockets in different parts on the lens panel or even side panels are not fitted by Rollei. As this was a WWII camera, almost all examples have German exposure tables on the back, calibrated in metres. Some cameras numbered on cast nameplate; others number engraved above nameplate. Due to shortage of materials some cameras chromium plated, others nickel plated. Variations in exposure table to include 100 ASA film.

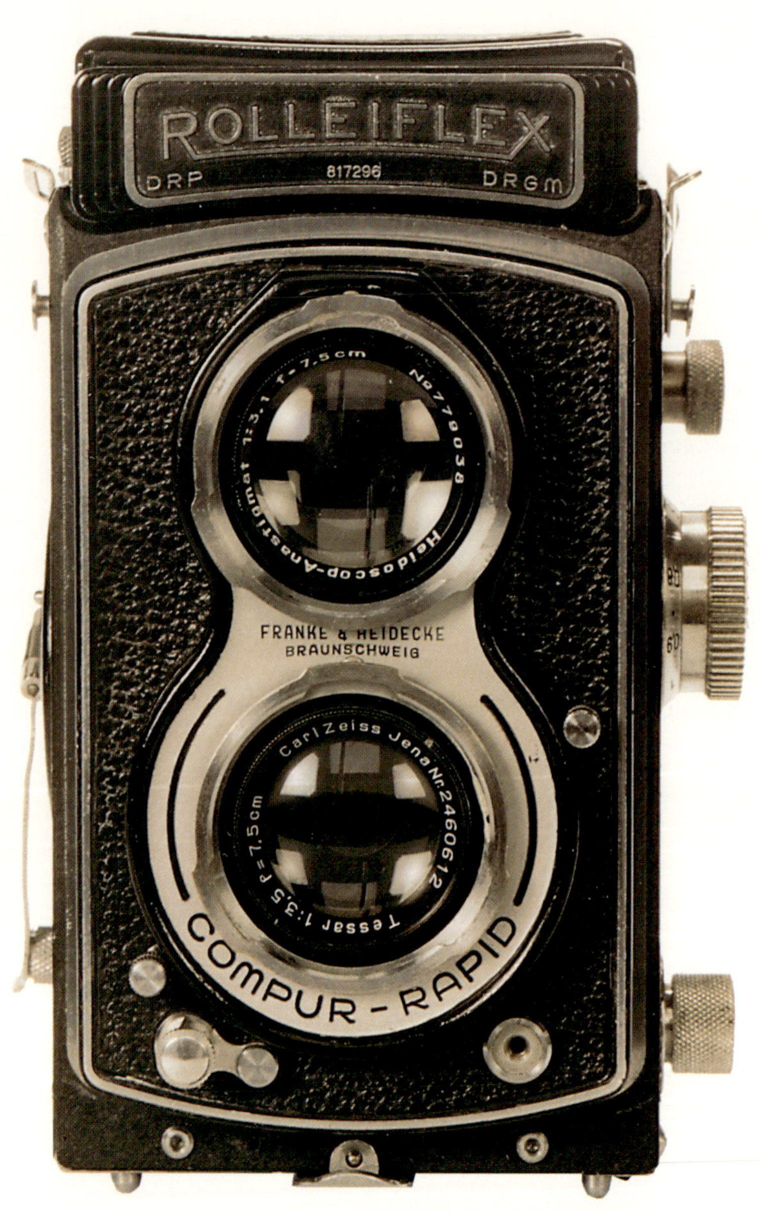

1939 New Standard Rolleiflex
No. K4 - 640

New Standard Rolleiflex

Factory Model
New Standard 6 x 6 K4 - 640

Launch Date
01-02-1939

Factory Termination Date
June 1941

Serial Numbers
805,000 - 927,999

Taking Lens
Carl Zeiss Jena Tessar
f3.5/75mm

Finder Lens
Heidoscop-Anastigmat
f3.1/75mm

Shutter
F.Deckel-Compur
Rapid

Speeds
1 - 1/500, B

Filter Size
Bayonet 1

Film Size
120 or 35mm with Rolleikin

Dimensions
14 x 9 x 9.5cm

Weight
876g

Launch Price Germany RM205 USA $130.00
UK £26.25

Identification

Both lenses accept Bayonet filters, small levers are placed on either side of the taking lens to adjust speed or aperture. A red window is used to position the first exposure, thereafter this is automatically operated by a cranking lever which also cocks the shutter. There is no delay timer.

Variations

There are different language versions for exposure guide on camera back, the distance scale is calibrated in metres or feet. This was an economy model costing 15% less than the Automat. R. F. Hunter, the English importer, advertised the Automat and cheaper Rolleicords, with few standard cameras imported into the UK, but then there were only four months to go before the outbreak of WWII.

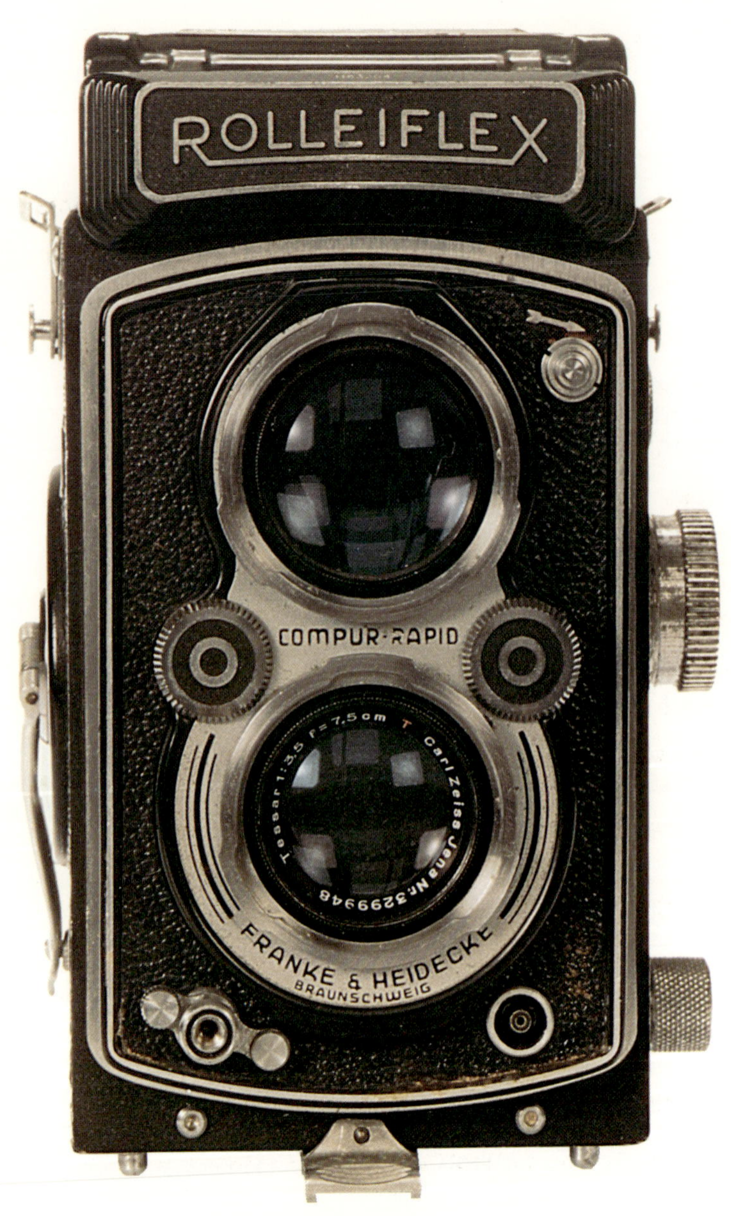

1945 Automat Rolleiflex
No. K4 B2 Model 3

Automat Rolleiflex Model 3

Factory Model
Automat 6x6 K4 B2

Launch Date
00-10-1945

Factory Termination Date
04-10-1949

Serial Numbers
1,050,000 - 1,099,999

Taking Lens
Carl Zeiss Jena Tessar
(see variations) f3.5/75mm

Finder Lens
Heidoscop-Anastigmat
f2.8/75mm

Shutter
F.Deckel-Compur Rapid

Speeds
1 - 1/500, B

Filter Size
Bayonet 1

Film Size
120 or 35 with Rolleikin

Dimensions
14 x 9 x 9.5cm

Weight
928g

Launch Price	Germany	RM400	USA	$265.00
	UK	Not Available		

Identification
Aperture and shutter control dials had a black inlay and not a grey one as in the previous model, "Compur - Rapid" logo is found between finder and taking lens, "Franke & Heidecke" name below taking lens. Shutter release is solid, without cable release.

Variations
Three lenses were available, the Carl Zeiss East German Jena Tessar throughout the production run, the West German Carl Zeiss Opton Tessar from February 1946, and the Schneider Xenar f3.5/75mm from July 1946. All taking lenses were factory coated. Synchronization was available as an option.

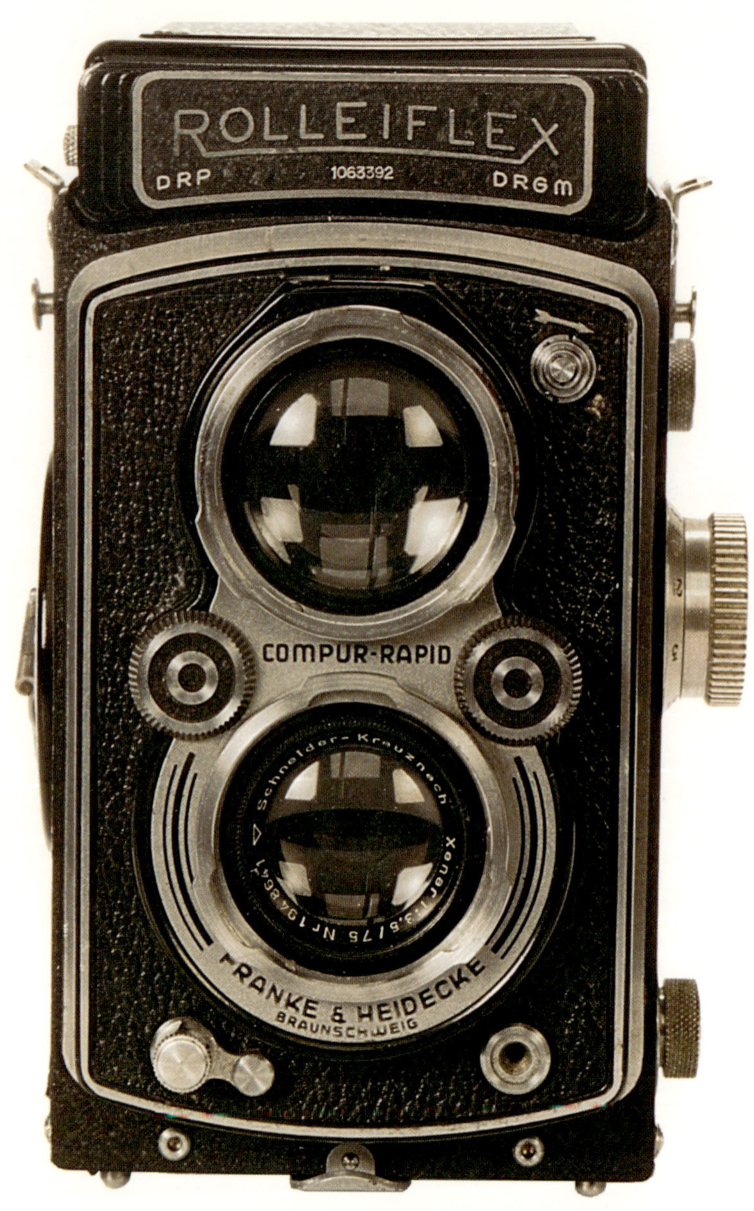

1949 Automat Rolleiflex Model X
No. K4 50

Automat Rolleiflex Model X

Factory Model
Automat 6x6 K4 Model 50

Launch Date
05-10-1949

Factory Termination Date
10-05-1951

Serial Numbers
1,000,000 - 1,168,000

Taking Lens
Zeiss Jena Tessar f3.5/75mm
Zeiss Opton Tessar f3.5/75mm
Schneider Xenar f3.5/75mm

Finder Lens
Heidoscop-Anastigmat
f2.8/75mm

Shutter
F.Deckel-Compur Rapid

Speeds
1 - 1/500, B

Filter Size
Bayonet 1

Film Size
120 or 35mm with Rolleikin

Dimensions
14.3 x 9 x 9.5cm

Weight
965g

Launch Price

Germany	DM398	USA	$235.00
UK	£121.00		

Identification

With standard X Synchronization cable release incorporated in shutter release socket. New type hood with large magnifier and 2 point accessory holder to hold masks built into the frame sports finder. 12 sec. delay timer. Tessar lens T coated; Xenar lens also coated with red triangle kite mark.

Variations

There is a 3 point accessory holder on the hood from No. 1,117,000 and adjustable pressure plate for Rolleikin II. Exposure tables in different languages. Focusing knob for export model engraved 'Made in Germany' in white letters, calibrated in feet.

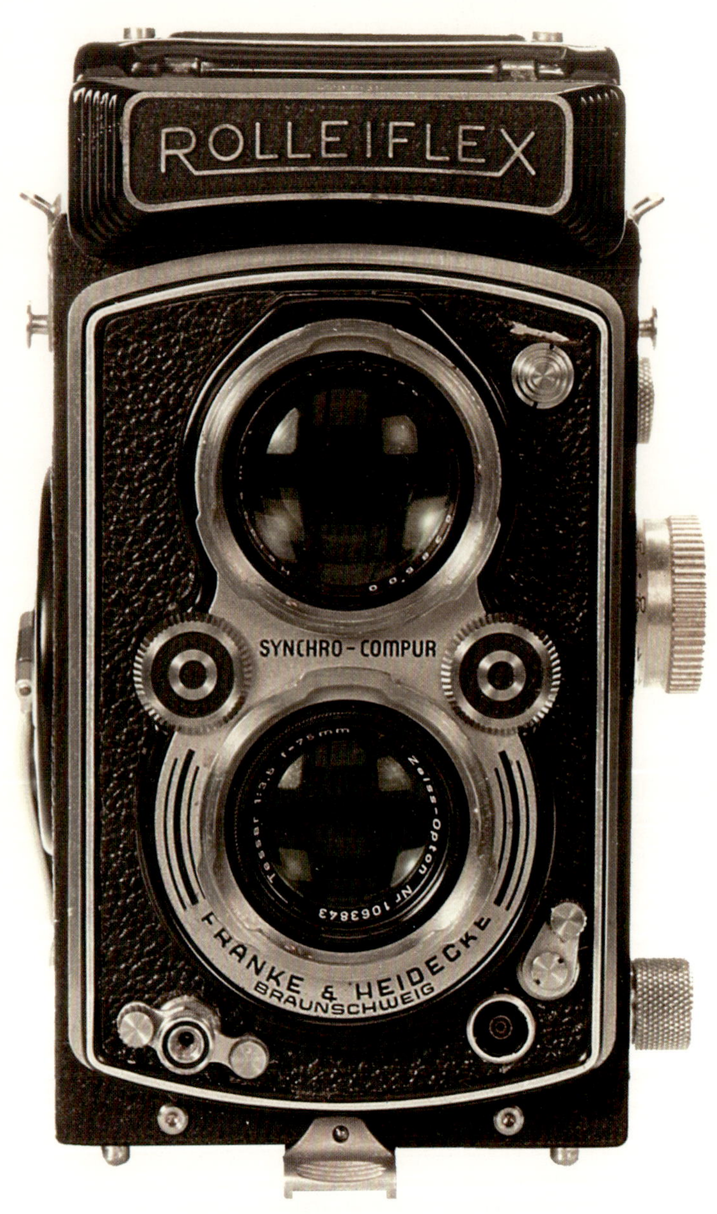

1951 Automat Rolleiflex
No. 6x6 K4A Model 4

Rolleiflex Automat Model 4

Factory Model
Automat 6x6 (K4A)

Launch Date
11-05-1951

Factory Termination Date
31-03-1954

Serial Numbers
1,200,000 - 1,427,999

Taking Lens
Carl Zeiss Jena Tessar f3.5/75mm
Carl Zeiss Opton Tessar f3.5/75mm
Schneider Xenar f3.5/75mm

Finder Lens
Heidoscop-Anastigmat f2.8/75mm

Shutter
F.Deckel-Synchro-Compur

Speeds
1 - 1/500, B

Filter Size
Bayonet 1

Film Size
120 or 35 with Rolleikin

Dimensions
14.3 x 9 x 9.5cm

Weight
970g

Launch Price Germany DM510 USA $235.00
UK £122.50

Identification

From the 1 February,1954, West German Zeiss lenses were known as Zeiss Opton, used in the last production batch. From No.1,267,000 a base plate was fitted with a groove to accept a quick release shoe or pistol grip.

Variations

Fitted with MX synchronization on the bottom right-hand side. The "Synchro - Compur" name is between the lenses. Exposure scale on camera back in different languages. Exposure knob for export model calibrated in metres or feet and etched 'Made in Germany' in white lettering.

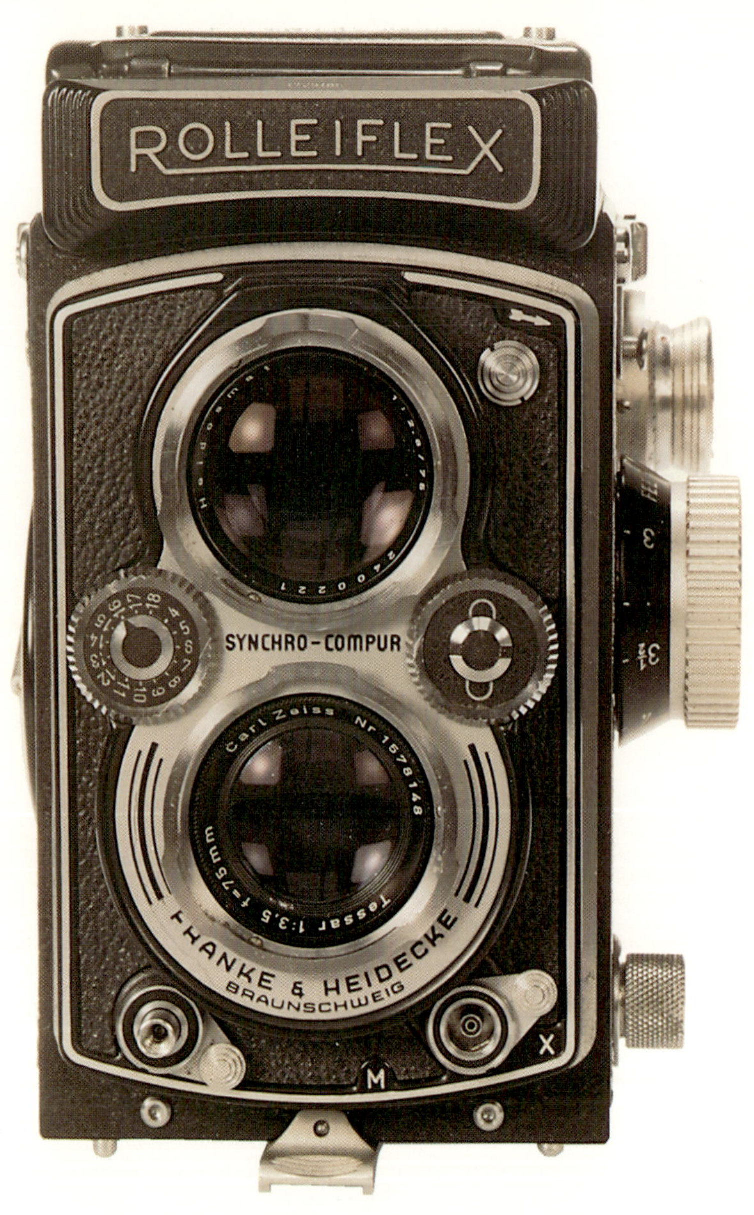

1954 Rolleiflex 3.5 MX-EVS No. K4B

Note right wheel with two half moons to lock EVS system

Rolleiflex 3.5 MX-EVS

Factory Model
Rolleiflex 3.5 6x6 (K4 B)
With EVS

Launch Date
29-03-1954

Factory Termination Date
12-09-1956

Serial Numbers
1,428,001 - 1,479,999 (Type 1)
1,479,000 - 1,739,999 (Type 2)

Taking Lens
Carl Zeiss Jena Tessar f3.5/75mm
Carl Zeiss Opton Tessar f3.5/75mm
Schneider Xenar f3.5/75mm

Finder Lens
Heidoscop-Anastigmat
f2.8/75mm

Shutter
F.Deckel-Synchro-Compur

Speeds
1 - 1/500, B

Dimensions

Weight
980g

Launch Price Germany DM530 USA $250.00
UK £137.65

Identification
MX Sync, EVS System whereby your hand-held meter EV reading could be locked into the Exposure Value System and thus by turning the wheel both aperture and shutter speed would correspond to the set EV scale. Large distance focus knob. Note new style neck strap lug, lower spool holder knob.

Variations
Type 1 - To disengage EVS hold down inner button of the aperture wheel with EV numbers. Type 2 - The EV system can be used coupled or uncoupled by changing the indent on the aperture wheel. Line up to two half circles for coupled. Type 1 aperture wheel with "Germany" on outer ring on prototype.
Serial numbers - Rollei allocated 33,000 numbers for what was to become a very popular camera. Various numbers were taken from other camera numbers between 1,479,001 - 1,739,999. It is believed that total production of this model was 65,000.

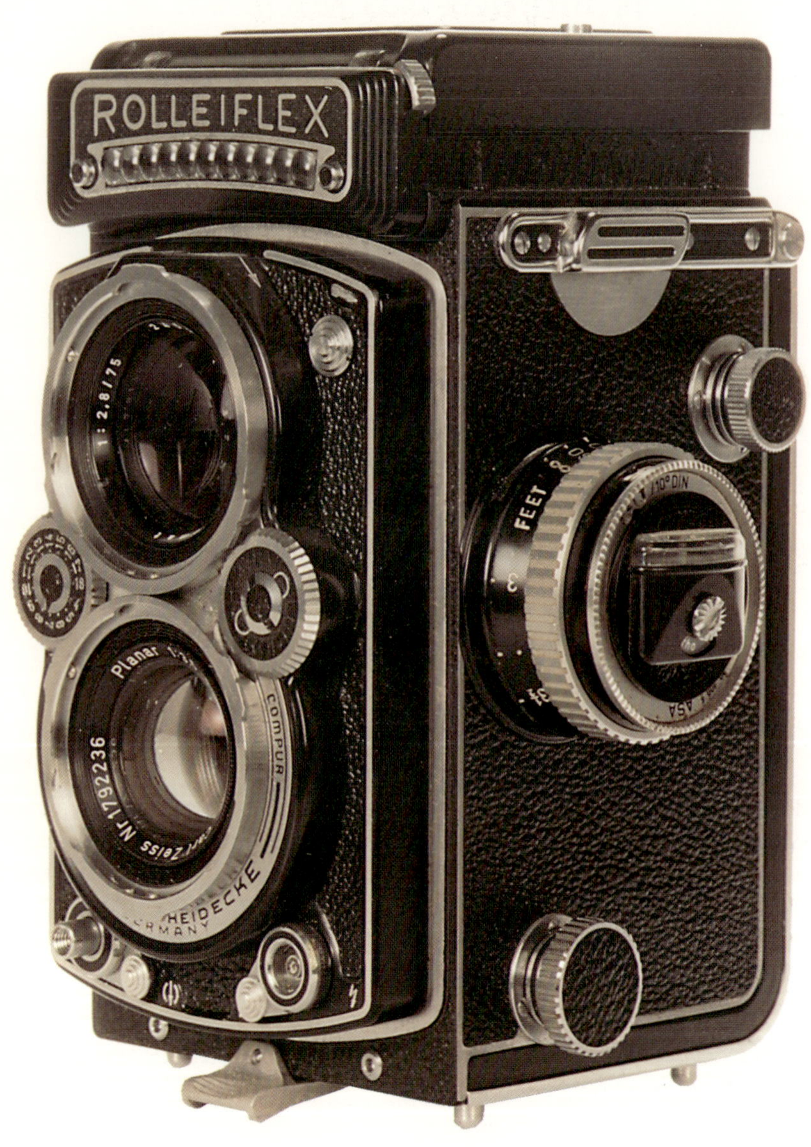

1956 Rolleiflex 3.5E
No. K4C

Rolleiflex 3.5 E

Factory Model
Rolleiflex 3.5 (K4C)

Launch Date
03-09-1956

Factory Termination Date
17-02-1959

Serial Numbers
1,740,000-1,787,849
(with lightmeter)
1,850,000-1,868,442
(without lightmeter)

Taking Lens
Carl Zeiss Planar f3.5/75mm
Schneider Xenotar f3.5/75mm

Finder Lens
Heidoscop-Anastigmat
f2.8/75mm

Shutter
F.Deckel-Synchro-Compur

Speeds
1 - 1/500, B

Filter Size
Bayonet II

Film Size
120 or 35mm with Rolleikin

Dimensions
14.6 x 7.5 x 9.6cm

Weight
1120g

Launch Price	Germany	RM605/550	USA	$272/229
	UK	£142.50/119.95		

Identification

Only 3.5 Rolleiflex with Zeiss Planar or Schneider Xenotar with non-removable hood (unless you use a screwdriver), and model number, i.e. 3.5E, does not precede the serial number. Camera back with exposure meter scale even if no factory meter was fitted.

Variations

At first with factory fitted exposure meter. A budget model without exposure meter, but which could be fitted later, appeared in 1958, see Serial Numbers. Camera was wired for meter, which is easily installed. This model with red dot mark by DBGM for meter switch. Focus knob calibrated in metres or feet.

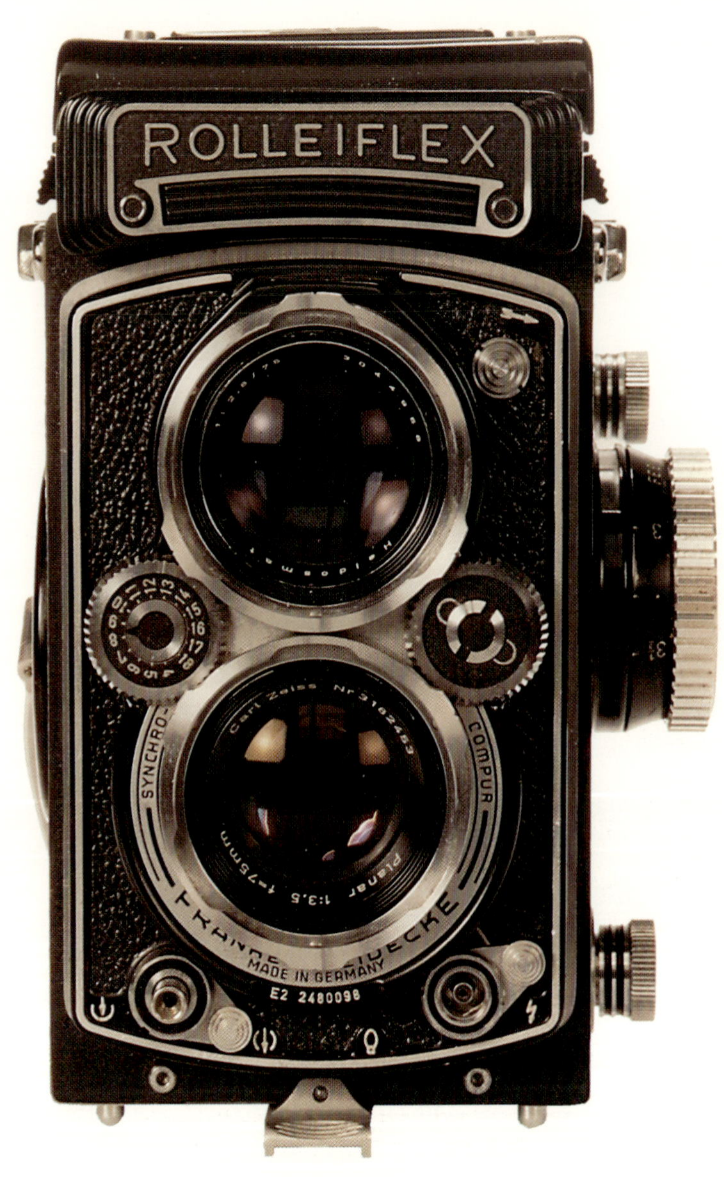

1959 Rolleiflex 3.5 E2
No. K4C3
Note serial number

Rolleiflex 3.5 E2

Factory Model
K4C2 & K4C3

Launch Date
07-12-1959
04-04-1960

Factory Termination Date
13-06-1961
10-05-1962

Serial Numbers
1,870,000 - 1,872,010 (K4C2)
2,480,000 - 2,482,999 (K4C3)

Taking Lens
Carl Zeiss Planar f3.5/75mm (K4C2)
Schneider Xenotar f3.5/75mm (K4C3)

Finder Lens
Heidosmat
f2.8/75mm

Shutter
Deckel Synchro
Compur MXV

Speeds
1 - 1/500, B

Filter Size
Bayonet II

Film Size
120 or 35mm with Rolleikin

Dimensions
14.6 x 7.5 x 9.6cm

Weight
1120g

Launch Price Germany Not available
UK Not available
USA $199.95

Identification
These models were a special order for the American Department and Mail Order firm Brooks, Ponder & Best. The 5,000, plus 10 samples, were mainly sold in the USA but through their mail order business many overseas and USA personnel helped in world distribution. The camera is numbered E2+ serial number below the taking lens. Unlike previous model, E2 had a removable hood. Different scale on camera back. Focusing knob calibrated in feet.

Variations
The first order was for Planar lens cameras using unsold 3.5E cameras with the number engraved below the taking lens as on the Rolleiflex T. The 3.5F went on sale in December 1958 and this was an opportunity of moving obsolescent stocks, becoming a collector's dream.

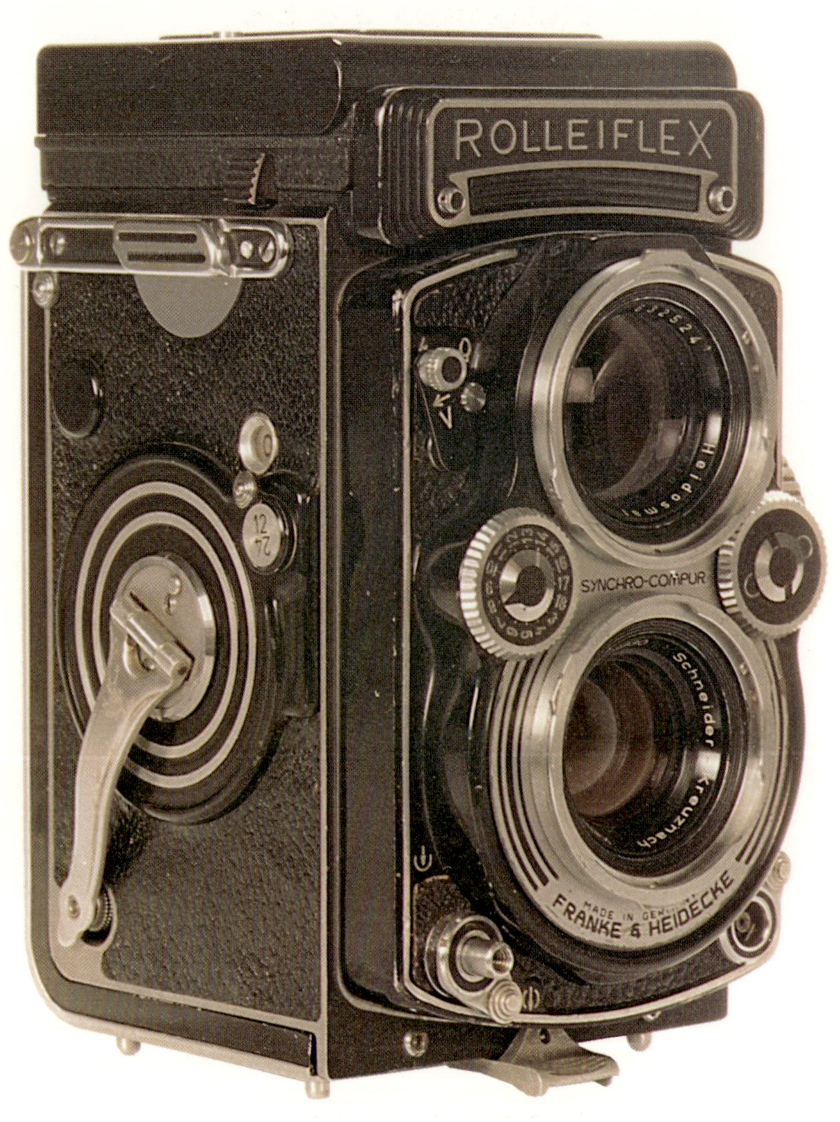

1961 Rolleiflex 3.5 E3
No. K4C3
Note serial number not under taking lens

Rolleiflex 3.5 E3

Factory Model
K4 C3

Launch Date
12-06-1961

Factory Termination Date
18-01-1965

Serial Numbers
2,380,000 - 2,385,034

Taking Lens
Zeiss Planar f3.5/75mm
Schneider Xenotar f3.5/75mm

Finder Lens
Heidosmat
f2.8/75mm

Shutter
Deckel Synchro
Compur MXV

Speeds
1 - 1/500, B

Filter Size
Bayonet II

Film Size
120, 220 or 35mm with Rolleikin

Dimensions
14.8 x 11.2 x 10.2

Weight
1180g

Launch Price	Germany	DM700Xenotar	USA	$240.00	Xenotar
		DM760 Planar		$250.00	Planar
	UK	Not available from UK importers			

Identification

3.5E3 precedes the serial number located front of hood. The words Synchro-Compur between lens, not in previous E camera. Note this camera is similar to the 3.5 F Model 2. The E3 has EVS scale on right speed dial whereas the 3.5F has no numbers. Note self timer on 3.5 E3 incorporated into MX lever beside finder lens. Although no factory installed meter, a T type meter could be fitted.

Variations

This camera had puzzled many collectors. It was primarily sold to studio photographers who wanted the EV scale found on their Weston exposure meters and also the 220 option that was available. The camera was otherwise identical to the 3.5F model 2. The Jersey Photographic Museum has the 220 version. Main sales were to South Americans who would buy the camera at a discount to the published list price.

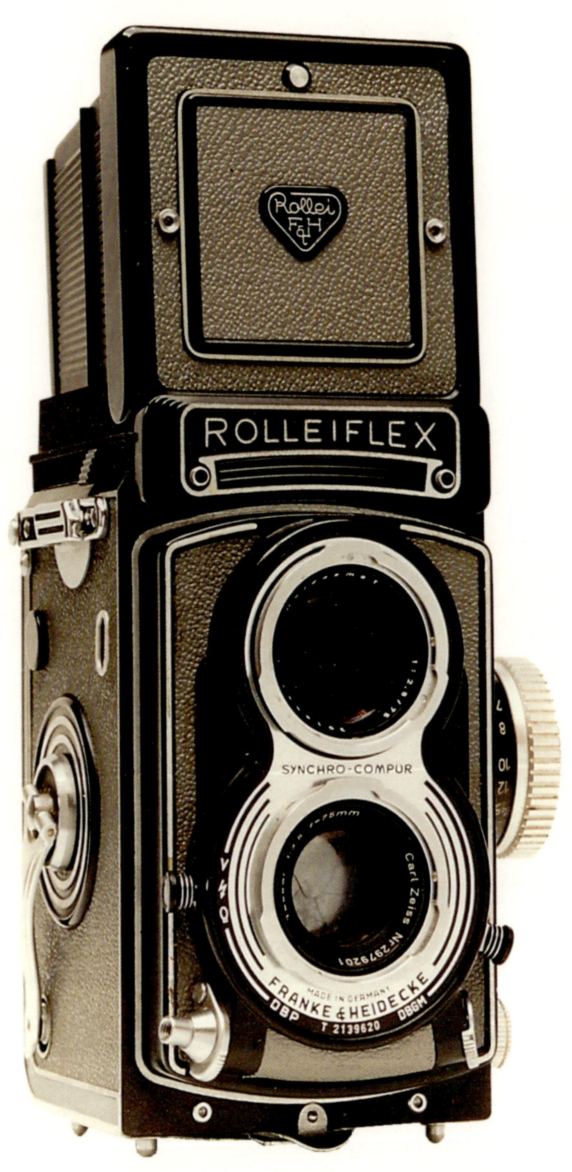

1958 Grey Rolleiflex T No. K8T

Note black plastic knobs to adjust aperture and shutter

Rolleiflex T 1

Factory Model
K8 T

Launch Date
12-09-1958

Factory Termination Date
10-09-1966

Serial Numbers
T 2,100,000 - T 2,199,999

Taking Lens
Carl Zeiss Tessar
f3.5/75mm

Finder Lens
Heidosmat
f2.8/75mm

Shutter
Deckel Synchro
Compur MXV

Speeds
B, 1, 1/2, 1/4, 1/8, 1/15, 1/30, 1/60, 1/125, 1/250, 1/500

Filter Size
Bayonet 1

Film Size
120 or 35mm with Rolleikin

Dimensions
14.8 x 10 x 9.5cm

Weight
1020g

Launch Price Germany DM444 USA $169.59 UK £75.00

Identification
The Rollei T serial number is preceded by the letter T and is located below the taking lens. Features include removable hood, black plastic levers to control aperture, speed or EVS scale. Type I has Synchro-Compur (without X) between lens and Franke & Heidecke.

Variations
Later models with Rollei-Werke. Until 1960 the T only available in grey leather to differentiate between the Rolleicord and Rolleiflex 3.5E. Later model I was available in black. A light meter could be fitted as an option as well as a removable hood.

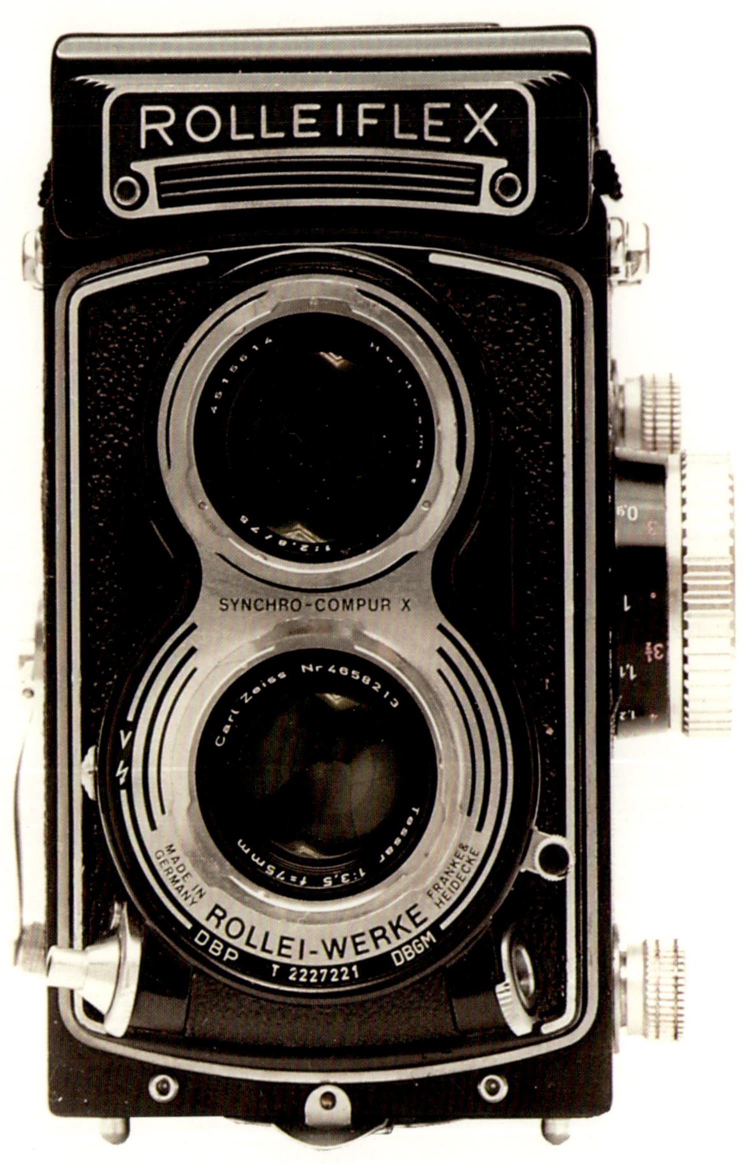

1966 Rolleiflex T2
_No. K8T2_
Note levers for adjusting aperture and shutter speed

Rolleiflex T 2

Factory Model
K8 T2

Launch Date
11-09-1966

Factory Termination Date
05-09-1971

Serial Number
T2,220,000 - T2,313,999

Taking Lens
Carl Zeiss Tessar
f3.5/75mm

Finder Lens
Heidosmat
f2.8/75mm

Shutter
Deckel Synchro Compur X

Speeds
B, 1, 1/2, 1/4, 1/8, 1/15, 1/30, 1/60, 1/125, 1/250, 1/500

Filter Size
Bayonet 1

Film Size
120 or 35mm with Rolleikin

Dimensions
14.8 x 10 x 9.5cm

Weight
1020g

Launch Price Germany DM500 USA $169.50 UK £117.00

Identification
The Rollei-Werke name below the taking lens replaces the Franke & Heidecke name. Metal levers for aperture, speed and EVS scale replaces black plastic as Model T1. Synchro-Compur name between lens with "x" and chrome half moon plate below strap lug omitted. Focusing knob now calibrated in metres and feet. M for flash bulb setting omitted with or without light meter. There were only a small number of grey cameras made to a special order in 1966.

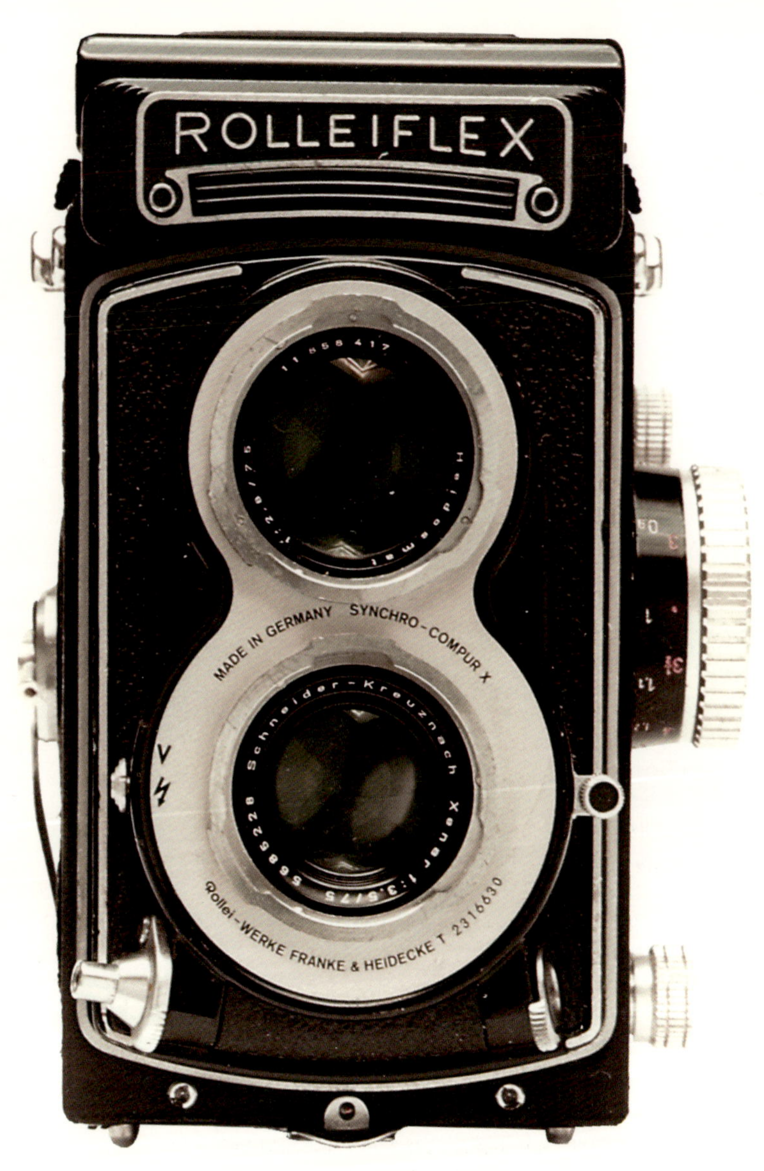

1971 Rolleiflex T3
No. K8T3
Note "white faced" lens panel

Rolleiflex T 3

Factory Model
K8T3

Launch Date
06-09-1971

Factory Termination Date
00-10-1976

Serial Numbers
T 2,314,000 - 2,320,298
(See "Identification" note)

Taking Lens
Carl Zeiss Tessar
f3.5/75mm

Finder Lens
Heidosmat
f2.8/75mm

Shutter
Deckel Synchro
Compur X

Speeds
B, 1, 1/2, 1/4, 1/8, 1/15, 1/30,
1/60, 1/125, 1/250, 1/500

Filter Size
Bayonet 1

Film Size
120 or 35mm with Rolleikin

Dimensions
14.8 x 10 x 9.5cm

Weight
1020g

Launch Price Germany DM535.21 USA $245.00 UK £171.10

Identification

"White Face" Rollei T with 'Rollei-Werke Franke & Heidecke' followed by number at bottom of taking lens. Thicker black leather with larger grain. The last Rolleiflex T is in the Jersey Photographic Museum, has no factory number but Xenar lens No. 11863983. It is said that No. T 2,320,449 is in the USA but factory records show No. T 2,320,298 as being the last serial number.

Variations

From No. T2,315,800 (approx.) taking lens f3.5/75mm Schneider Xenar.

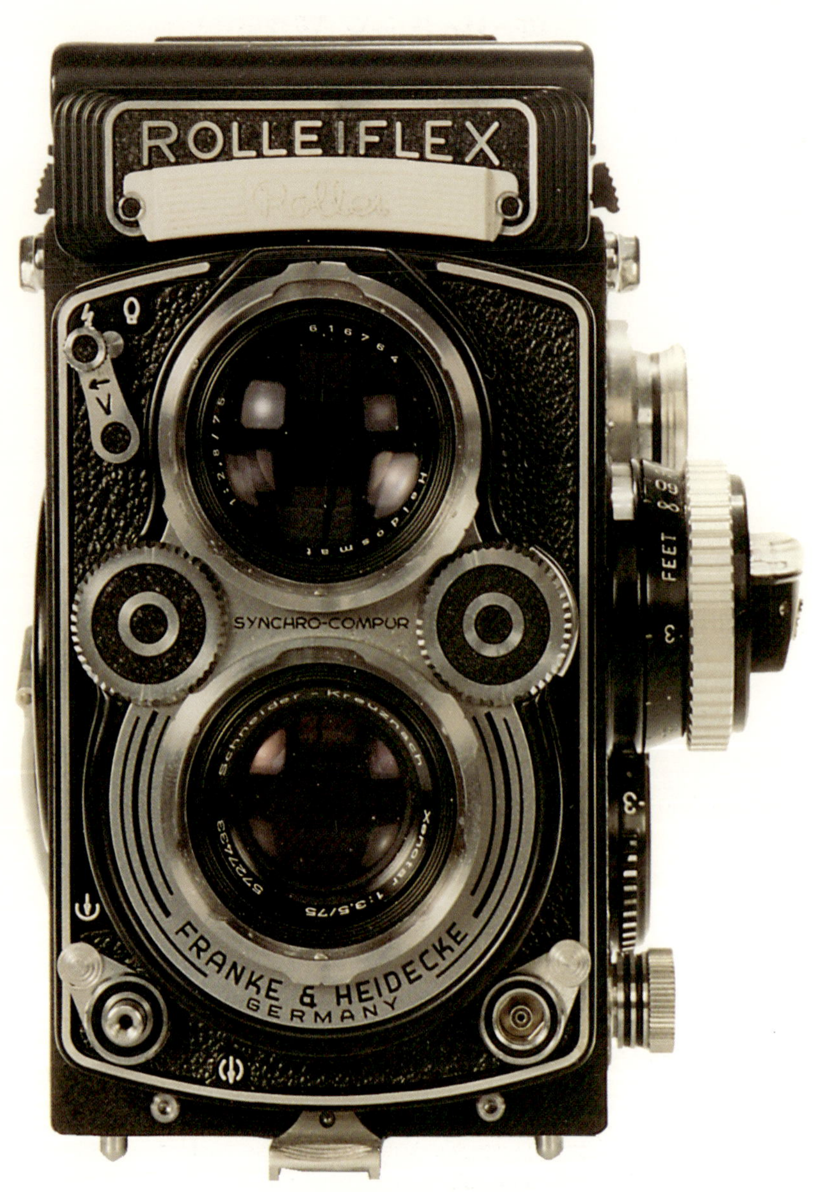

1958 Rolleiflex 3.5F Model 1
No. K4D

Rolleiflex 3.5F Model 1

Factory Model
No. 6x6 K4D

Launch Date
12-12-1958

Factory Termination Date
30-01-1960

Serial Numbers
2,200,000 - 2,219,999

Taking Lens
Zeiss Planar f3.5/75mm
Schneider Xenotar f3.5/75mm

Finder Lens
Heidosmat
f2.8/75mm

Shutter
Deckel Synchro-Compur
MXV

Speeds
1 - 1/500, B

Filter Size
Bayonet II

Film Size
120 accepts Rolleikin for 35mm

Dimensions
14.5 x 10.5 x 10cm

Weight
1220g

Launch Price	Germany	DM648	USA	$250.00
	France	FF1375	UK	£106.00

Identification
3.5F precedes camera number above nameplate except for first production. Removable hood. Top left corner electric sign for flash gun synchronization, small bulb sign for bulb flashguns and "v" on positioning lever for shutter delay. Half moon metal plate below strap lug. This is omitted on later models 4 & 5.

Variations
The camera is available with either a Zeiss Planar 5 element lens or Schneider Xenotar lens. Distance scale either calibrated in metres or feet. Camera supplied with or without meter.

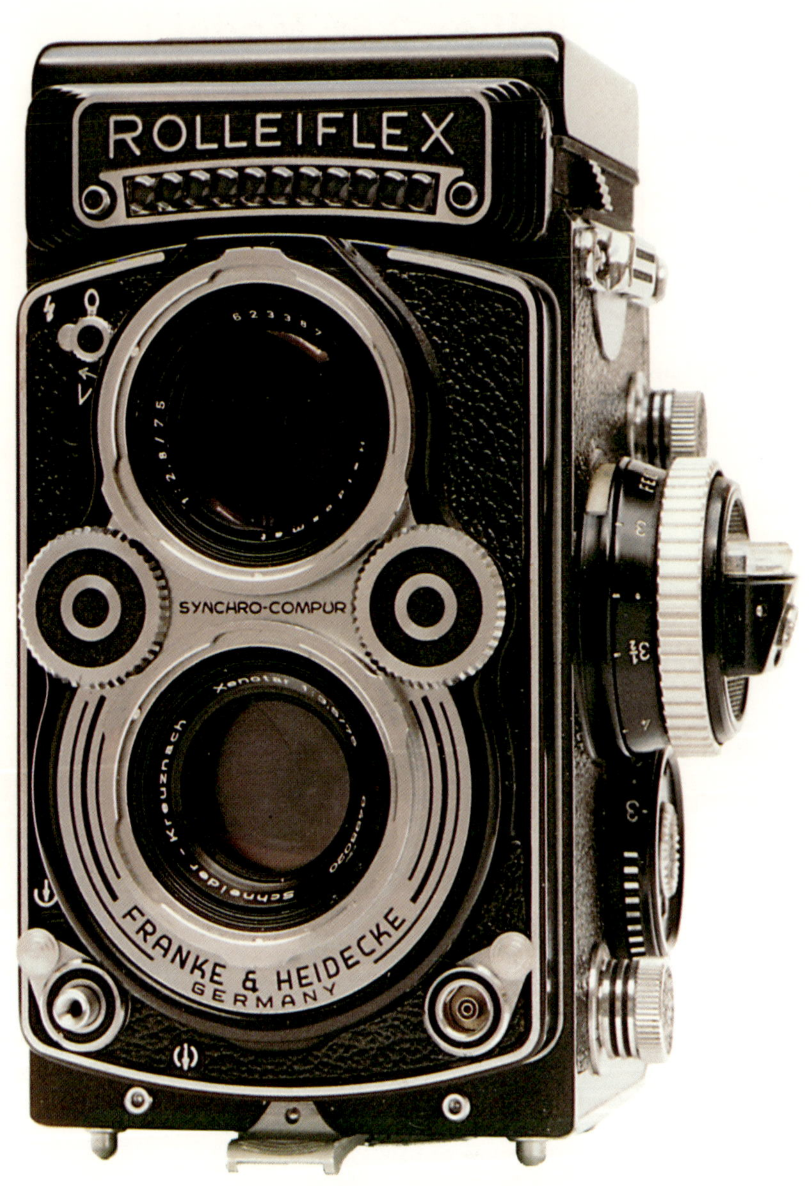

1960 Rolleiflex 3.5F Model 2
No. K4E

Rolleiflex 3.5F Model 2

Factory Model
No. 6x6 K4E

Launch Date
01-02-1960

Factory Termination Date
12-11-1960

Serial Numbers
2,230,000 - 2,241,500

Taking Lens
Zeiss Planar f3.5/75mm
Schneider Xenotar f3.5/75mm

Finder Lens
Heidosmat
f2.8/75mm

Shutter
Deckel Synchro-Compur
MXV

Speeds
1 - 1/500, B

Filter Size
Bayonet II

Film Size
120 accepts Rolleikin for 35mm

Dimensions
14.5 x 10.5 x 10cm

Weight
1220g

Launch Price

Germany	DM648	USA	$250.00
France	FF1375		

UK	£119.45	Planar with meter
	£110.40	Xenotar with meter

Identification
Internal release pin to accept optical glass pressure plate to ensure film is flat. Shutter speeds on models No. 1 and 2 are located on the outside of the peep window with aperture on the inside. This is reversed on models 3, 4 and 5. Models No. 1 and 2 name below taking lens "Franke & Heidecke Germany". Later models named "Made in Germany Franke & Heidecke", otherwise as model No. 1.

Variations
Model 2 available with or without meter, Zeiss Planar or Schneider Xenotar lens, distance scale in metres or feet.

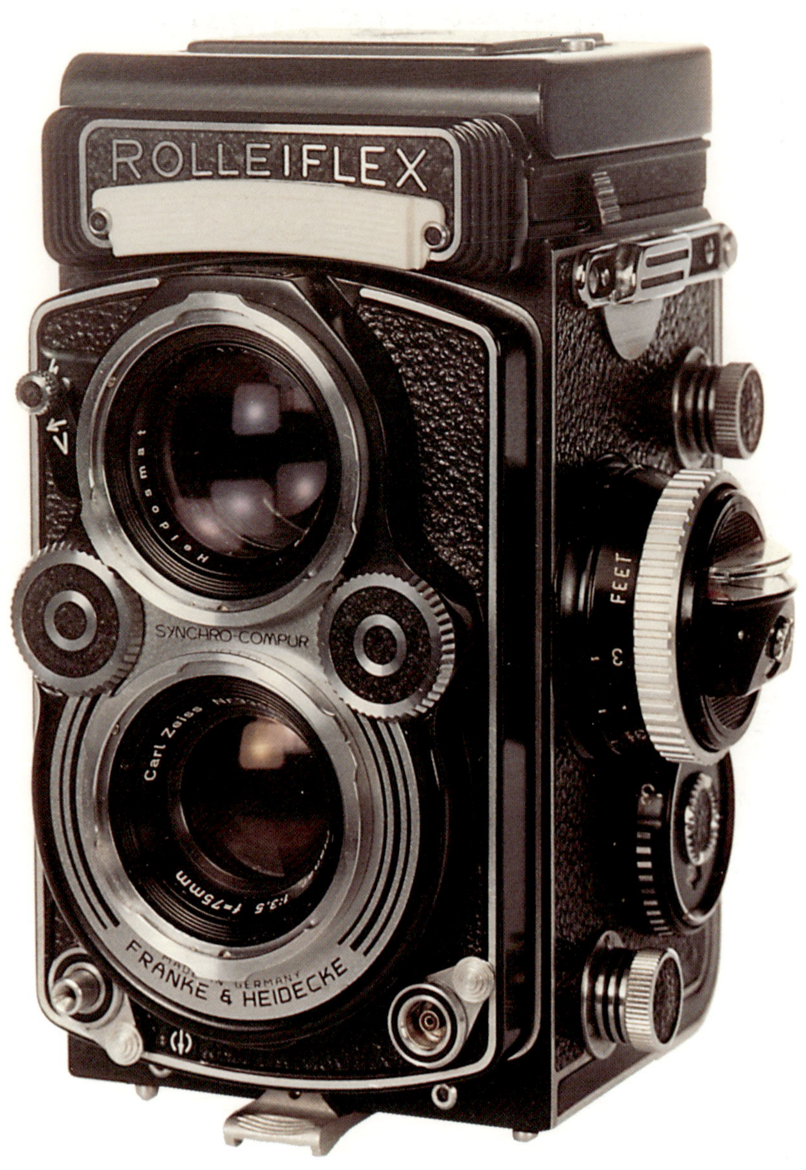

1960 Rolleiflex 3.5F Model 3
No. K4F

Rolleiflex 3.5F Model 3

Factory Model
K4F

Launch Date
15-09-1960

Factory Termination Date
23-12-1964

Serial Numbers
2,250,000 - 2,299,999

Taking Lens
Zeiss Planar f3.5/75mm
Schneider Xenotar f3.5/75mm

Finder Lens
Heidosmat
f2.8/75mm

Shutter
Deckel Synchro-Compur
MXV

Speeds
1 - 1/500, B

Filter Size
Bayonet II

Film Size
120 Accepts Rolleikin for 35mm

Dimensions
14.5 x 10.5 x 10cm

Weight
1120g

Launch Price	Germany	DM760	USA	$269.00
	UK	£127.65		

Identification

Company name under taking lens, "Made in Germany" above "Franke & Heidecke". Whereas on model Nos. 1 & 2 the word "Germany" is below "Franke & Heidecke". From model No. 2,298,816 the distance scale is incorporated in both metres and feet. All model 3 cameras with optical glass release pin, see model 2.

Variations

Cameras available with Zeiss Planar or Schneider Xenotar lens, with or without exposure meter.

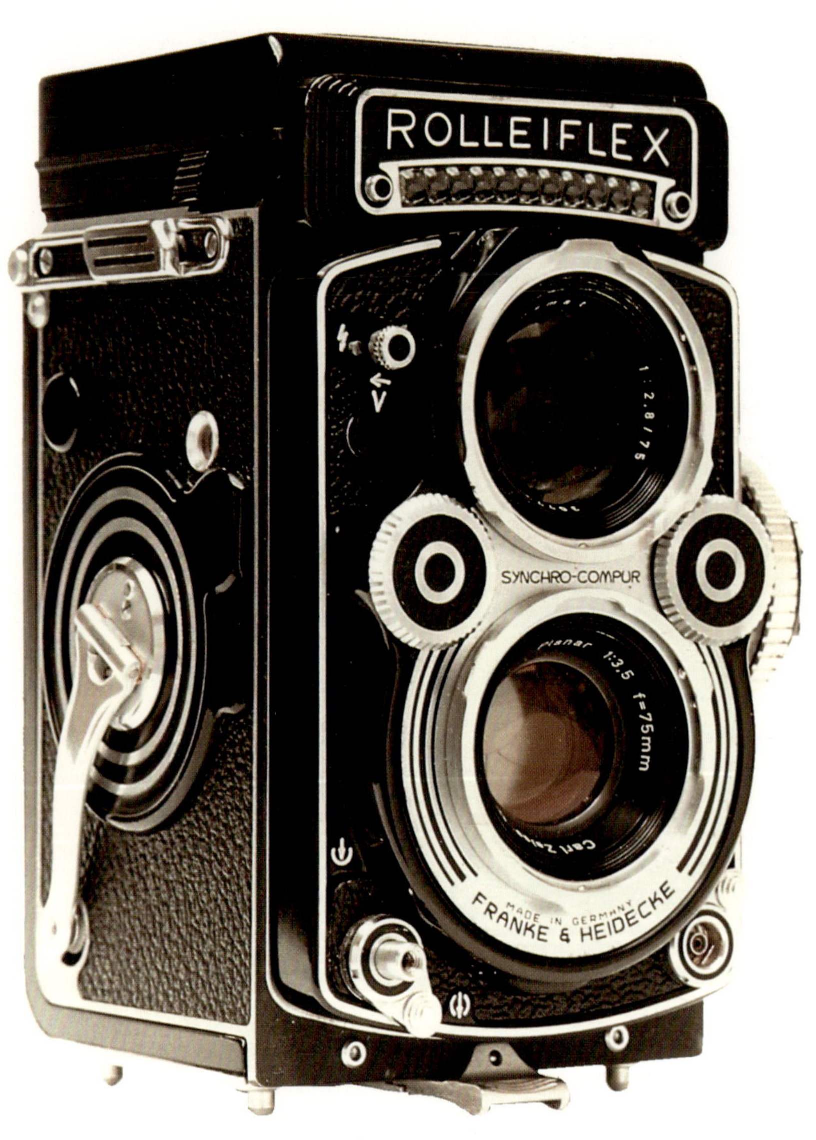

1965 Rolleiflex 3.5F Model 4
No. K4F/1
Note 12/24 panel above lever wind

Rolleiflex 3.5F Model 4

Factory Model
K4F/1

Launch Date
04-01-1965

Factory Termination Date
00-12-1976

Serial Numbers
2,800,000 - 2,844,999

Taking Lens
Schneider Xenotar f3.5/75mm
Carl Zeiss Planar f3.5/75mm

Finder Lens
Heidosmat
f2.8/75mm

Shutter
Deckel Synchro
Compur MXV

Speeds
1 - 1/500, B

Filter Size
Bayonet II

Film Size
120 or 35mm with Rolleikin

Dimensions
14.8 x 11.2 x 10.5cm

Weight
1120g

Launch Price	Germany	DM750 Planar	USA	$269.00 Planar
		DM698 Xenotar		$249.50 Xenotar
	UK	£157.30 Planar		
		£163.25 - with 220 option		

Identification
Serial number preceded by 3.5F. Half moon chrome plate below strap lug discontinued. 220 built in panel below film counter. Distance scale in feet and metres.

Variations
The camera was normally sold with a meter and was available with either a Planar or Xenotar lens.

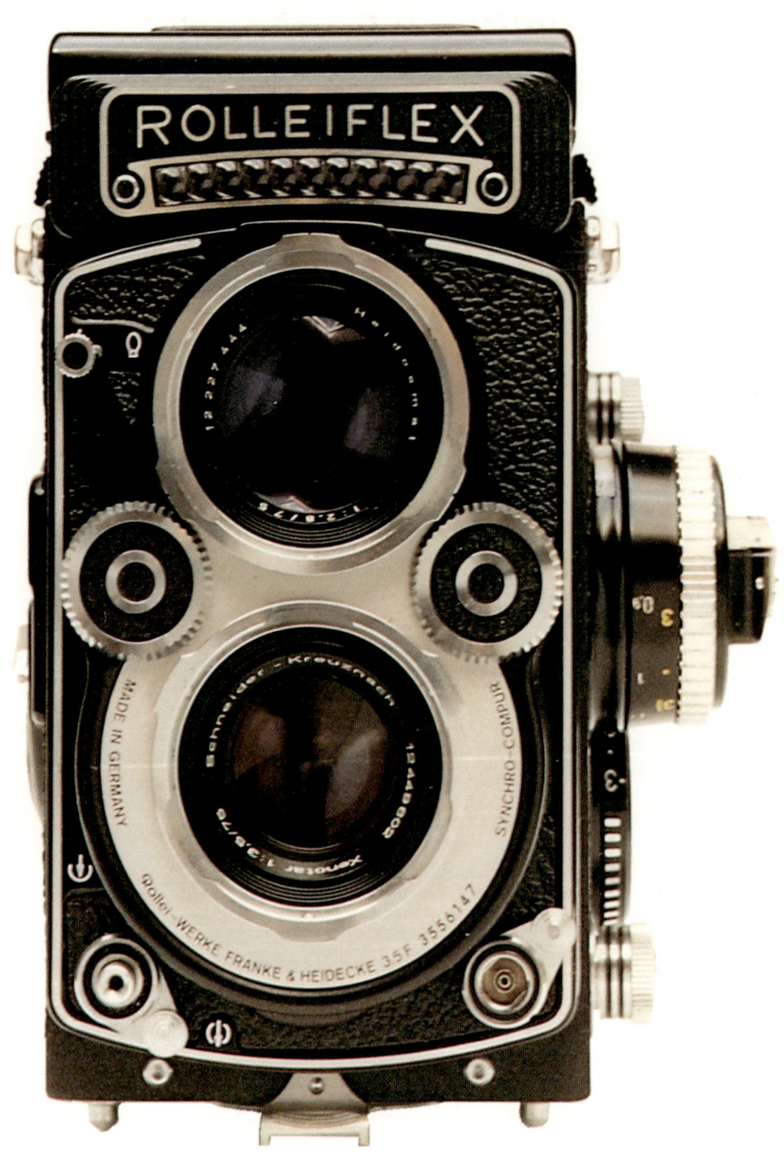

1979 Rolleiflex 3.5F Model 5
_No. K4F/2_
Note new company name under taking lens

Rolleiflex 3.5F Model 5

Factory Model
6x6 K4F/2

Launch Date
January 1979

Factory Termination Date
December 1979

Serial Number
2,845,000 - 2,857,149
3,555,000 - 3,559,999

Taking Lens
Schneider Xenotar f3.5/75mm
Zeiss Planar f3.5/75mm

Finder Lens
Heidosmat
f2.8/75mm

Shutter
Deckel Synchro - Compur
MXV

Speeds
1 - 1/500, B

Filter Size
Bayonet II

Film Size
120 accepts Rolleikin for 35mm
220 with 12/24 option

Dimensions
14.8 x 11.2 x 10.5cm

Weight
1120g

Launch Price	Germany	DM700	USA	$400.00
	France	FF8000	UK	£351.00

Identification
Model 5 120/220 option. This facility permits 24 exposures on 220 film: original additional cost £13.50. Camera number located beneath taking lens. New company name under taking lens, "Rollei-Werke Franke & Heidecke". Some reports give final number for first series as 2,870,149.

Variations
From a user's point of view there is no difference between the Planar or Xenotar lens. The first and last models were Xenotar lensed. Some misleading information quotes termination date 1976. For collectors there are six variations with Planar 120, name change and again with Xenotar lenses.

Are you getting the best from your Rollei?

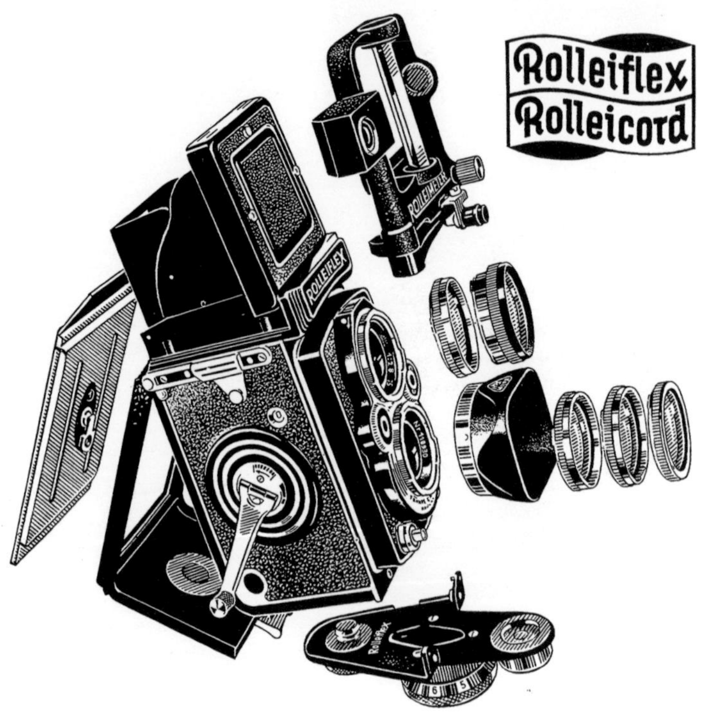

There is an incomparable range of accessories for your Rollei camera. Do you know them all, their purpose and how they will help you to get even better results with your Rollei? Go to your dealer and study the range of accessories and have them demonstrated to you. The great majority of these accessories are freely available and can be imported without restriction.

IT IS MOST IMPORTANT TO NOTE THE FOLLOWING:

Optical accessories such as filters, supplementary lenses, soft focus lenses, lens hoods, etc., will in future be marketed with bayonet mounts in **three** diameters:

1. For Tessar, Triotar and Xenar f/3.5;
2. For Planar and Xenotar f/3.5;
3. For Planar and Xenotar f/2.8.

This applies also to the Rolleiflash flashgun which is affixed to the top bayonet mount **on Rollei cameras.**

Rolleiflex 2.8f

In 1949 Rollei celebrated the completion of the 500,000th Rolleiflex camera. Paul Franke, who died a year later was not feeling well and did not attend the celebration in Rollei's canteen. Reinhold Heidecke and Paul Franke's son Horst, together with a number of senior staff, decided to celebrate in style with a litre bottle of beer and some ham and cheese rolls.

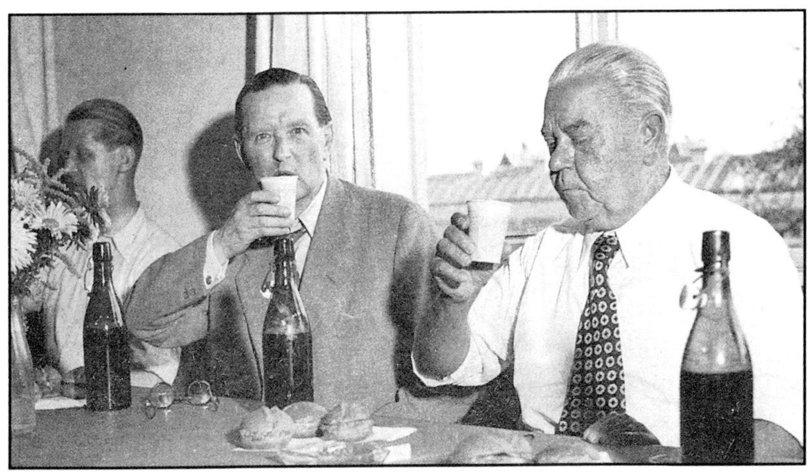

A few months later, in October 1949, the photographic media were treated to a buffet with wine when the 2.8A with f2.8/80mm lens was launched and almost sunk. This camera, hurriedly put into production to compete with other medium format cameras at that time, was a disaster.

The Tessar f2.8 lenses were manufactured during the war by Carl Zeiss Jena with serial numbers between 2,300,000 and 3,000,000. The lenses were faulty and gave a very soft image. It is said that they were originally made for a Zeiss 1941 Ikoflex IIIa. The 1939 Zeiss Ikoflex III twin lens reflex did have a f2.8/80mm Zeiss Tessar and a Compur Rapid shutter of 1/400 or 1/500. Deckel, manufacturers of the Compur shutter, was owned by Zeiss, and when Rollei wanted to compete with Hasselblad (who had in 1948 launched their 1600F, the world's first 6x6 SLR with interchangeable lenses and film magazines - the standard lens for the Hasselblad was a f2.8/80mm Kodak Ektar), Zeiss offered a package deal with a f2.8/80mm and 1/400 Compur Rapid shutter.

This solution to Rollei's requirement was too hasty and not well thought out, as the Compur Rapid shutter on the 3.5 Rolleiflex and Rolleicord at that time was 1/500th. The factory recalled the cameras for a lens change. The total production of the faulty lensed cameras was around 5000. The Jersey Photographic Museum's camera was acquired from a professional studio photographer who had retired. The camera was not one that had its lens changed over and he was very pleased with the soft results.

Today's 2.8GX Rollei TLR's are as they say, "the state of the art". Now with redesigned Planar lenses, HFT coated to improve contrast and reduce flare, these lenses are now made by Rollei. Rollei have come a long way since their disastrous entry into the f2.8 TLR camera market.

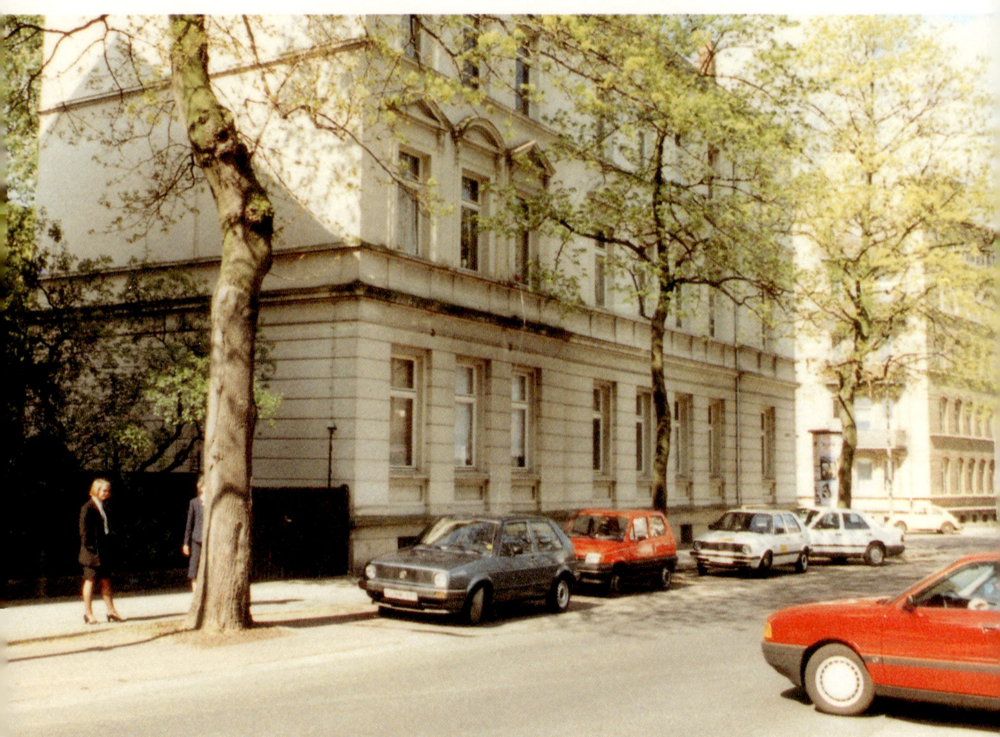

The original home of Rollei
No.32 Viewegstraße, Braunschweig

The Rolleiflex 2.8f

Serial Nos.	Model Type	Factory No.	Year	Page No.
1,101,000 - 1,114,999	2.8A Type 1	(K7A)	1949	121
1,115,000 - 1,139,999	2.8A Type 1	(K7A)	1949	121
1,154,000 - 1,163,999	2.8A Type 2	(K7A)	1951	123
1,201,000 - 1,201,999	2.8A Type 2	(K7A)	1951	123
1,204,000 - 1,259,999	2.8B	(K7B)	1952	125
1,260,000 - 1,457,405	2.8C	(K7C)	1952	127
1,600,000 - 1,620,100	2.8D	(K7D)	1955	129
1,621,000 - 1,664,999	2.8E	(K7E)	1956	131
2,350,000 - 2,356,999	2.8E2	(K7E2)	1959	133
2,360,000 - 2,362,024	2.8E3	(K7E3)	1962	135
2,400,000 - 2,451,850	2.8F	(K7F)	1960	137
2,451,851 - 2,479,999	2.8F2	(K7F2)	1966	139
2,600,000 - 2,799,999	2.8F3	(K7F3)	1969	139
2,900,000 - 2,959,999	2.8F4	(K7F4)	1976	141
7,570,001 - 7,571,249	Aurum	(K7FA)	1982	143
8,300,000 - 8,301,499	Aurum	(K7FA)	1983	143
2,985,000 - 2,985,499	Platin	(K7FP)	1984	145
2,986,500 - 2,986,599	Platin A	(K7FPA)	1989	145
2,985,500 -	2.8GX	(K7G)	1987	147
5,010,000 - 5,017,999	2.8GXED	(K7GE)	1989	151
6,030,000 - 8,036,999	2.8GXHN	(K7GHN)	1992	151
8,810,000 -	2.8GX	(K7G)	1993	

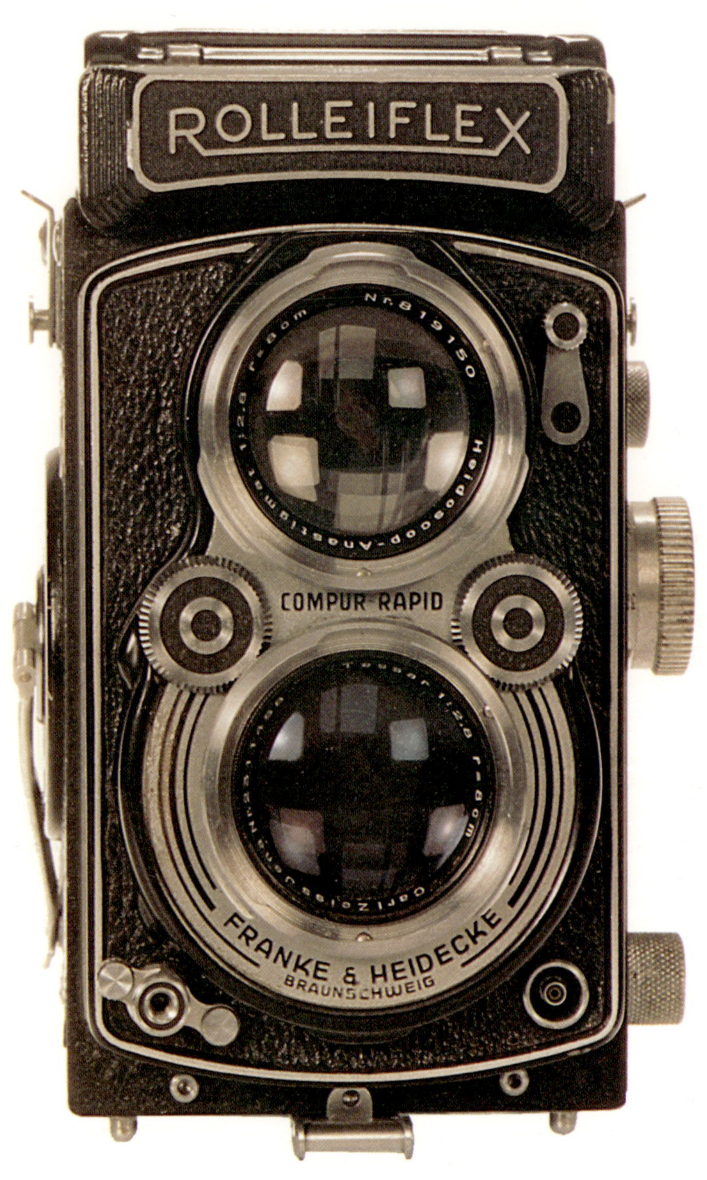

1949 Rolleiflex 2.8A Type 1
No. K7A
with original lens

Rolleiflex 2.8A Type I

Factory Model
K7A

Launch Date
31-10-1949

Factory Termination Date
24-02-1951

Serial Numbers
1,101,000 -1,114,999 Jena Tessar
1,115,000 -1,139,999 Opton Tessar

Taking Lens
Zeiss Jena Tessar f2.8/80mm
Zeiss Opton Tessar f2.8/80mm

Finder Lens
Heidoscop-Anastigmat
f2.8/80mm

Shutter
Deckel Compur-Rapid X

Speeds
1 - 1/500, B

Filter Size
Bayonet II

Film Size
120 or 35mm with Rolleikin

Dimensions
4.5 x 9 x 10.4cm

Weight
1067g

Launch Price Germany DM700 USA $325.00 UK £179.50

Identification

This is the first Rollei 6x6 TLR with f2.8 taking lens, and the only f2.8 camera with Bayonet II and top shutter speed of 1/400th. The type I did not have MX Synchronization, only X. Original 2.8A type I fitted with Carl Zeiss Jena Tessar lens No. 2,300,000 to 3,000,000 were recalled and fitted with Opton Tessar lens and the MX was added. A 2.8A with the MX letters above the delayed timer lever was a sure guide that the camera was a type 2 or had been upgraded.

Variations

Out of 13,000 cameras recalled only half were returned for modification. From serial No. 1,115,000 the camera was fitted with the Zeiss Opton lens and from serial No. 1,201,000 with MX. The distance scale could be in metres or feet and the exposure scale on the camera back can be found in different languages. The pressure plate is not adjustable and is unpainted on type I.

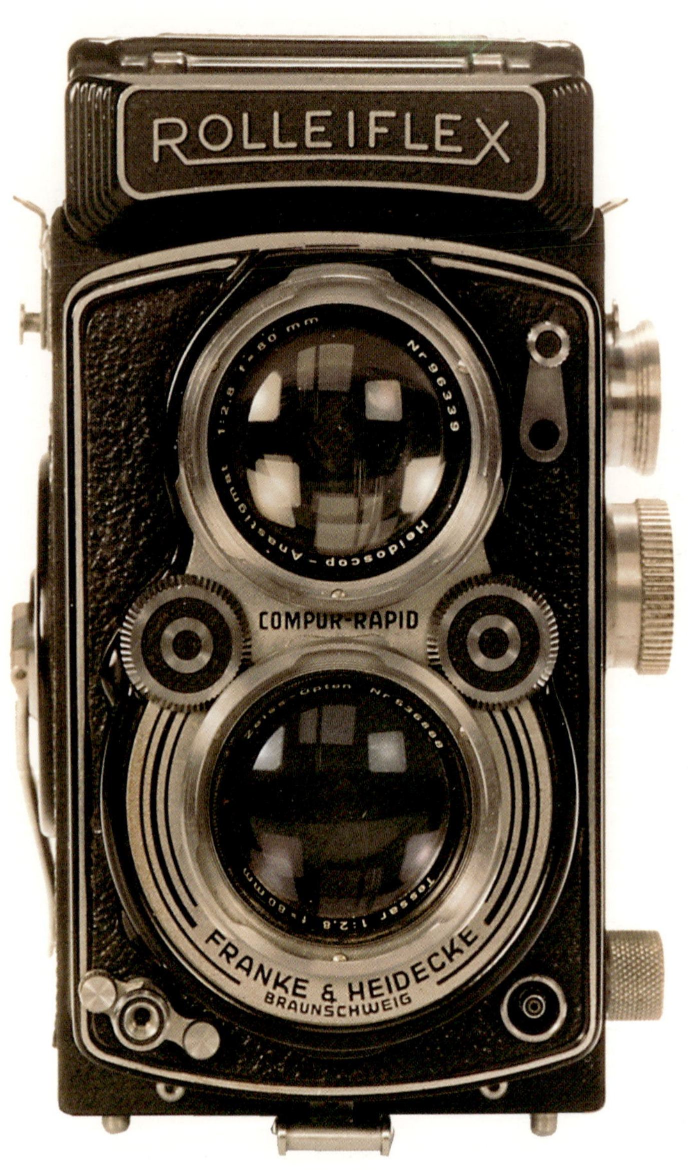

1951 Rolleiflex 2.8A Type 2
No. K7A
with Zeiss Opton Tessar lens

Rolleiflex 2.8A Type 2

Factory Model
K7A

Launch Date
24-02-1951

Factory Termination Date
29-09-1951

Serial Numbers
1,154,000-1,163,999 Shutter1/400th
1,201,000-1,201,999 Shutter1/500th

Taking Lens
Zeiss Opton Tessar
f2.8/80mm

Finder Lens
Heidoscop-Anastigmat
f2.8/80mm

Shutter
Deckel Compur
Rapid MX

Speed
1 - 1/400 or 1 - 1/500, B

Filter Size
Bayonet III

Film Size
120 or 35mm with Rolleikin

Dimensions
14.5 x 9 x 10.4cm

Weight
1067g

Launch Price Germany DM700 USA $325.00 UK £182.50

Identification
Black adjustable pressure plate and 1/400th second shutter 80mm lens. No EVS scale on aperture or speed dials. It is essential that the only sure way to identify this camera is by the camera's serial number due to modifications available. From serial No. 1,201,000 MX shutter with speeds to 1/500th.

Variations
Normal variations with distance scale in feet or metres and different language exposure tables on reverse. Three point accessory mask holder studs on hood. Bayonet II together with the smaller lens, often mistaken as a 3.5 Rolleiflex. Look carefully at the serial number.

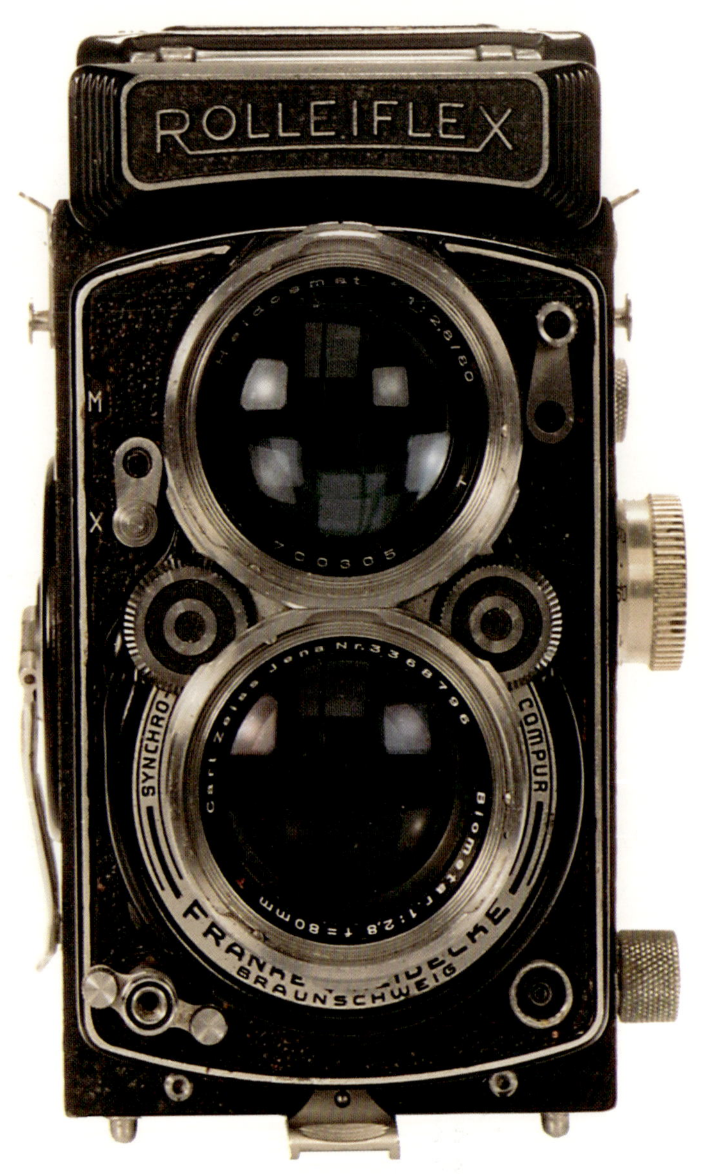

1952 Rolleiflex 2.8B
No. K7B
with Carl Zeiss Biometar lens

Rolleiflex 2.8B

Factory Model
K7B

Launch Date
23-08-1952

Factory Termination Date
30-05-1953

Serial Numbers
1,204,000 - 1,259,999

Taking Lens
Carl Zeiss Jena Biometar
f2.8/80mm

Finder Lens
Heidoscop-Anastigmat
f2.8/80mm

Shutter
Deckel Synchro

Speeds
1 - 1/500, B
Separate self timer

Filter Size
Bayonet III

Film Size
120 or 35mm with Rolleikin

Dimensions
14.5 x 9 x 10.4cm

Weight
1050g

Launch Price Germany DM750 USA $345.00 UK £189.95

Identification

The only Rolleiflex TLR to have a Zeiss Biometar lens. This was a stop gap camera to overcome the adverse publicity of the 2.8A. In Germany the 2.8C with Schneider Xenotar was available in 1952. The 2.8B was an export model sold mainly in North and South America. Note separate self timer also found on the 2.8C.

Variations

After Serial No. 1,241,000 the hood has a three point accessory mask holder and together with the 500th shutter speed remained with the Rollei TLR until the introduction of the 2.8GX.

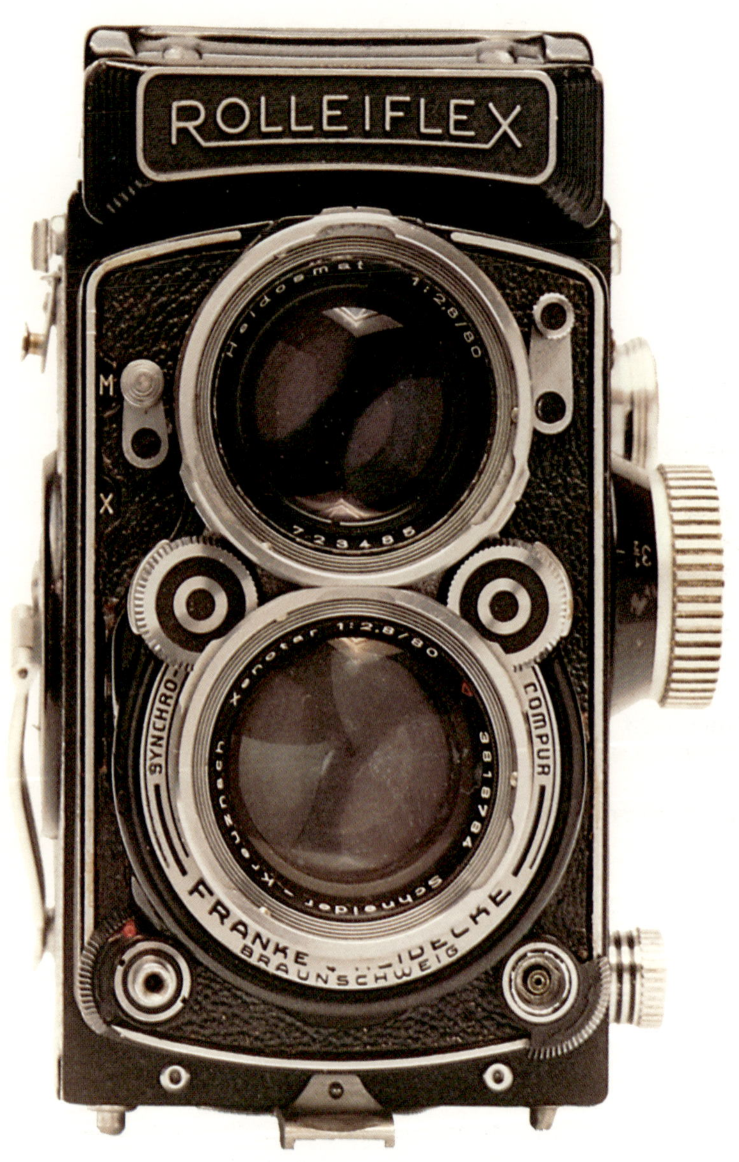

1952 Rolleiflex 2.8C
_No. K7C_
Note locking catches on aperture and shutter dials

Rolleiflex 2.8C

Factory Model
K7C

Launch Date
10-12-1952

Factory Termination Date
24-06-1955

Serial Numbers
1,260,000 - 1,457,405

Taking Lens
Carl Zeiss Planar f2.8/80mm
Schneider Xenotar f2.8/80mm

Finder Lens
Heidosmat
f2.8/80mm

Shutter
Deckel Synchro
Compur MX

Speeds
1 - 1/500, B
Separate self-timer

Filter Size
Bayonet III

Film Size
120 or 35mm with Rolleikin

Dimensions
14.5 x 10.5 x 10.4cm

Weight
1134g

Launch Price Germany DM750 USA $345.00 UK £147.08

Identification

Separate self timer; on future models this was included in the MX or MVX lever. No EVS scale as found in D and E models. Black plastic safety catch on shutter release and flash synchronization socket. This was replaced by metal on subsequent models as on the 2.8A and 2.8B.

Variations

At first only the Xenotar f2.8/80mm lens was available but from 30th March, 1954, the Carl Zeiss Planar option was available in Germany for an additional DM50 or $12 in the USA from serial No. 1,362,702.

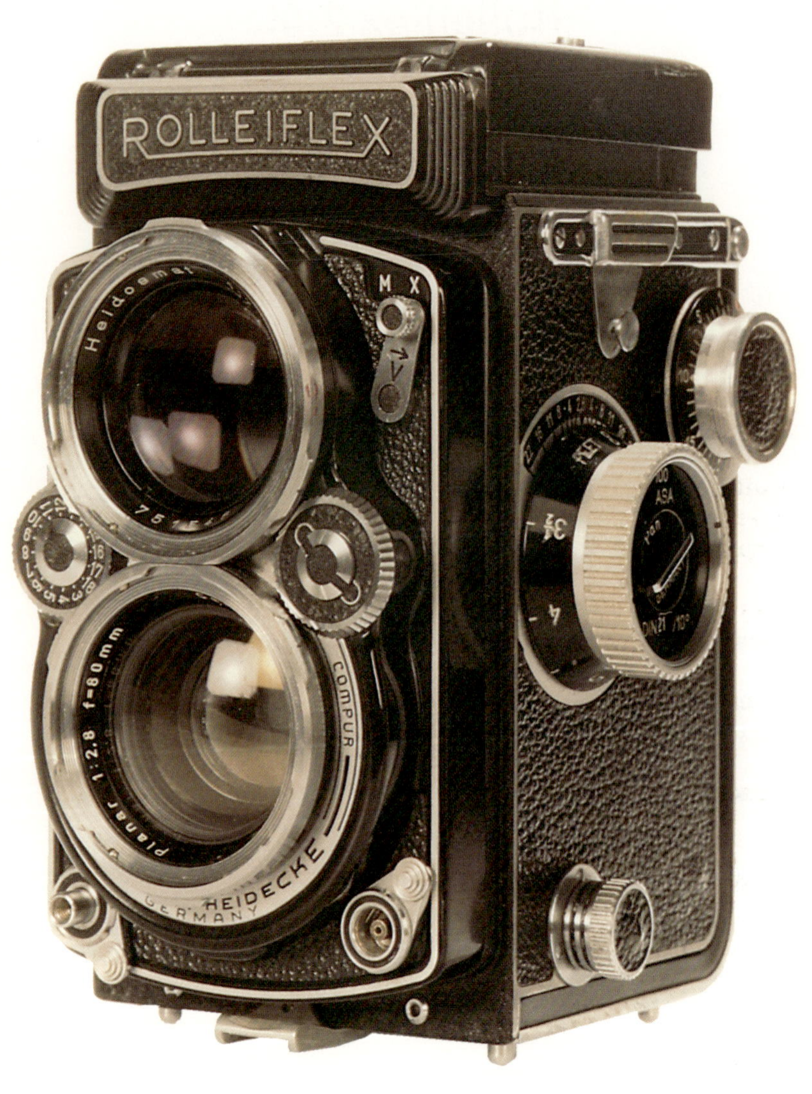

1955 Rolleiflex 2.8D
No. K7D
fitted with 35 counter

Rolleiflex 2.8D

Factory Model
K7D

Launch Date
20-07-1955

Factory Termination Date
12-09-1956

Serial numbers
1,600,000 - 1,620,100

Taking Lens
Carl Zeiss Planar f2.8/80mm
Schneider Xenotar f2.8/80mm

Finder Lens
Heidosmat
f2.8/80mm

Shutter
Deckel Synchro
Compur MX

Speeds
1 - 1/500, B

Filter Size
Bayonet III

Film Size
120 or 35mm with Rolleikin

Dimensions
14.5 x 10.5 x 10.4cm

Weight
1450g

Launch Price Germany DM720 USA $291.50 UK £129.85

Identification

EVS system calibrated right-hand dial that locked speed and aperture. To unlock, press left-hand aperture dial. Self timer incorporated on MX lever marked V. The exposure scale on the camera back is now in pictures and numerals thereby not requiring different languages on back for each country.

Variations

Both lenses were available from the launch date. The Zeiss Planar costing more than the Xenotar. First batch without V (self-timer) engraved on MX lever. All 2.8D appear to be fitted with 35mm Rolleikin counter. From Model No. 1,609,000 EVS scale coupled or uncoupled as on "E". Remember "D" model with fixed hood Some cameras with half moon scissor strap attachment.

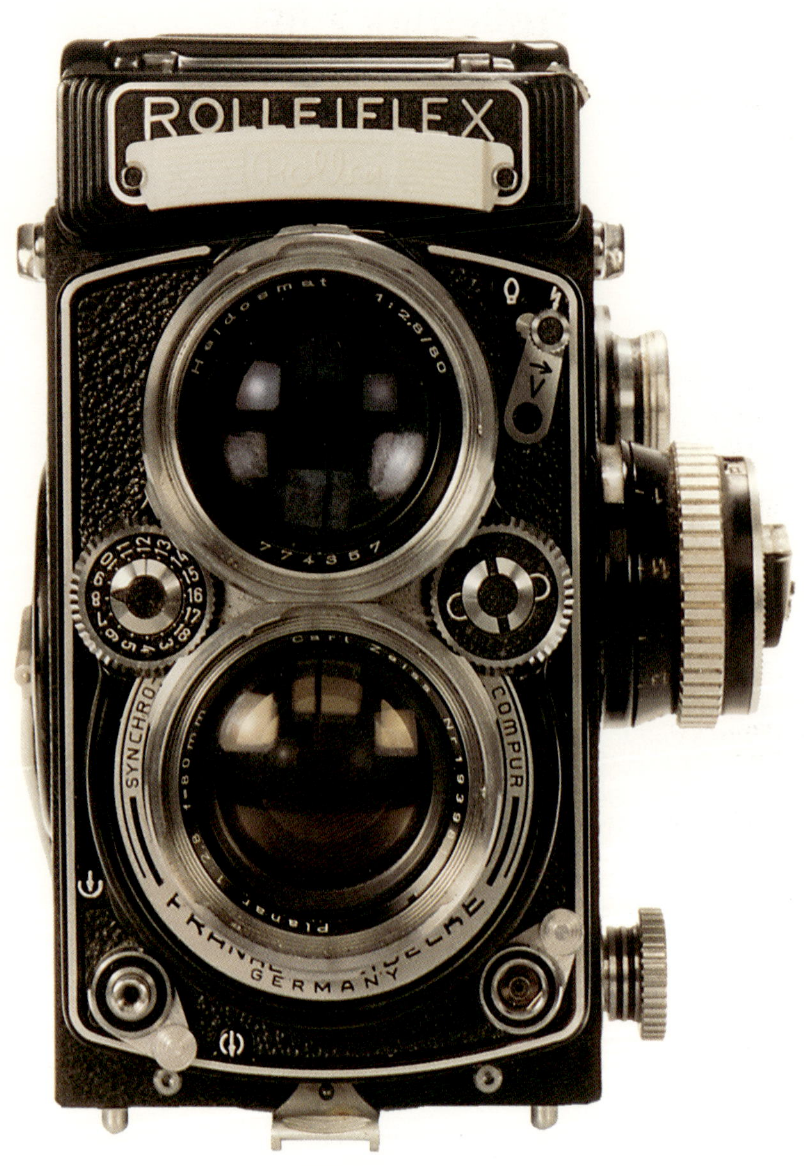

1956 Rolleiflex 2.8E
No. K7E

Rolleiflex 2.8E

Factory Model
K7E

Launch Date
10-09-1956

Factory Termination Date
30-09-1959

Serial Numbers
1,621,000 - 1,664,999

Taking Lens
Carl Zeiss Planar f2.8/80mm
Schneider Xenotar f2.8/80mm

Finder Lens
Heidosmat
f2.8/80mm

Shutter
Deckel Synchro
Compur MXV

Speeds
1 - 1/500, B

Filter Size
Bayonet III

Film Size
120 or 35mm with Rolleikin

Dimensions
14.8 x 10.5 x 10.4cm

Weight
1240g

Launch Price	Germany	DM820 Planar DM775 Xenotar	USA	$331.50 Planar $312.00 Xenotar
	UK	£129.50 Planar £122.50 Xenotar		

Identification
Half moon metal plate under scissor strap lug. MXV and EVS scales, large focusing knob, and double exposure facility. Depth of field scale contained in focusing knob.

Variations
Planar or Xenotar lens, distance scale on focusing knob in feet or metres. The Xenotar lensed camera without meter cost DM750, $312.95 and, in the UK, £109.80. All 2.8E seen by the author have 35mm counter and non-removable hood.

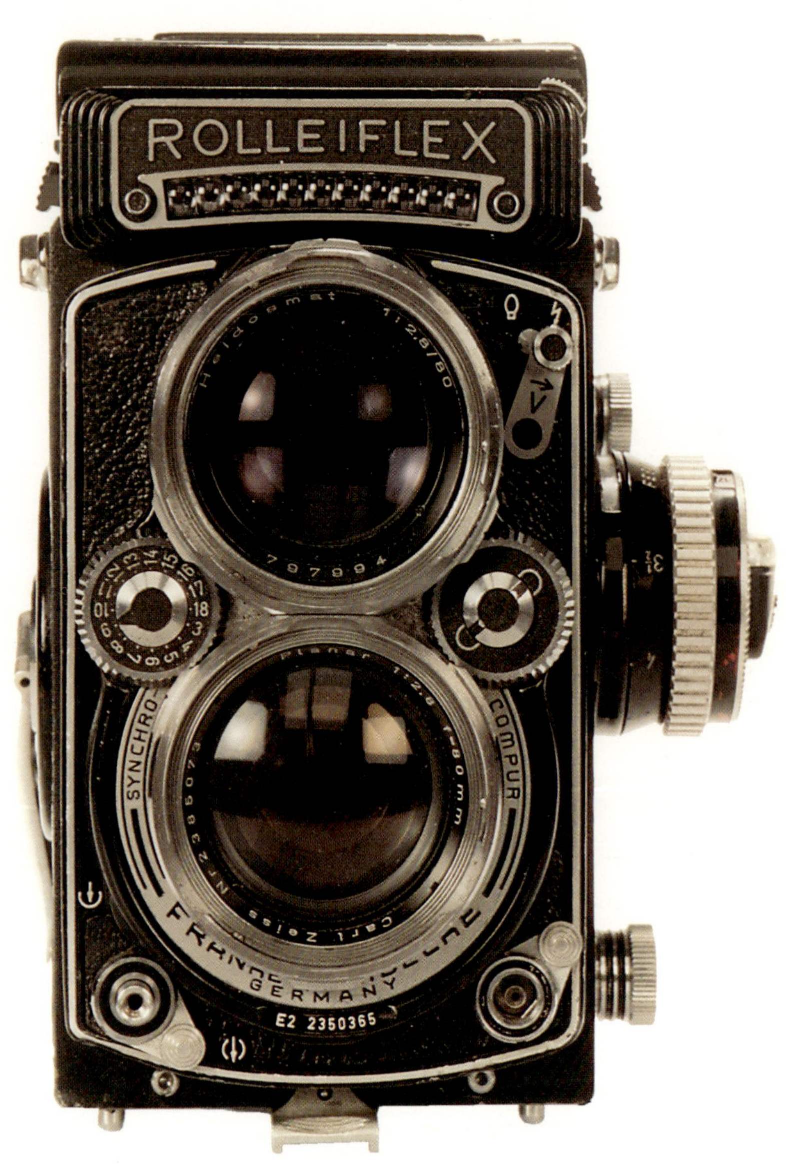

1959 Rolleiflex 2.8E2
_No. K7E2_
Note serial number below taking lens

Rolleiflex 2.8E 2

Factory Model	**Launch Date**
K7E2	24-08-1959
	Factory Termination Date
	00-06-1960
	Serial Numbers
	2,350,000 - 2,356,999

Taking Lens
Carl Zeiss Planar f2.8/80mm
Schneider Xenotar f2.8/80mm

Finder Lens
Heidosmat
f2.8/80mm

Shutter
Deckel Synchro
Compur MXV

Speeds
1 - 1/500, B

Filter Size
Bayonet III

Film Size
120 or 35mm with Rolleikin

Dimension
14.8 x 10.5 x 10.4cm

Weight
1280g

Launch Price	Germany	DM840 Planar	USA	$309.95 Planar
		DM796 Xenotar		$294.95 Xenotar
	UK	£140.30 Planar		
		£133.05 Xenotar		

Identification

E2 precedes the Serial Number below the taking lens. There is a removable hood to enable the use of a prism. The Rollei logo is on the hood. EVS scale could be uncoupled by turning inner wheel on aperture ring.

Variations

Choice of lens, Planar or Xenotar, and exposure meters. To avoid confusion with a multitude of similar models, Rollei placed the serial number and model number below the taking lens, for example the Rollei 3.5Tele and Wide-angle, and later the 2.8F.

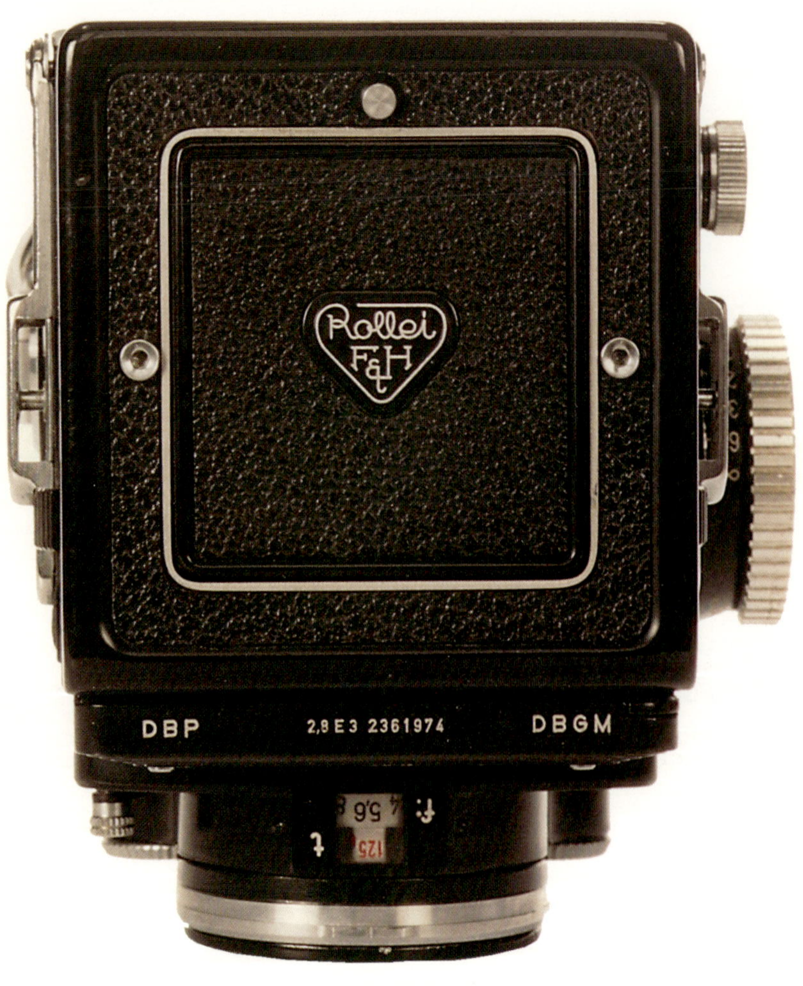

1962 Rolleiflex 2.8E3
No. K7E3
Picture shows studs on hood to hold 35mm masks and serial number

Rolleiflex 2.8E 3

Factory Model
K7E3

Launch Date
29-03-1962

Factory Termination Date
08-01-1965

Serial Numbers
2,360,000 - 2,362,024

Taking Lens
Zeiss Planar f2.8/80mm
Schneider Xenotar f2.8/80mm

Finder Lens
Heidosmat
f2.8/80mm

Shutter
Deckel Synchro
Compur MXV

Speeds
1 - 1/500, B

Filter Size
Bayonet III

Film Size
120 or 35mm with Rolleikin

Dimensions
14.8 x 10.5 x 10.4cm

Weight
1280g

Launch Price	Germany	DM880 Planar	USA	$320.00 Planar
		DM815 Xenotar		$307.00 Xenotar
	UK	Not imported by the UK agents.		

Identification

The serial number is located above the Rolleiflex name. No meter was supplied but this could be added at a later date for DM57.50 ($28.50). This camera was ordered by the USA store group Brooks, Ponder & Best for their mail order catalogue. This camera was not listed in the UK. It appeared on a 1961 German list for their domestic market. As this was a budget camera, sold at a special price to utilise unsold E2 parts, it is unlikely that any Planar lens camera existed. The Editors would like to hear from anyone with a 2.8E3 with a Planar lens.

Variations

Note the camera number is above the nameplate, see photo, whereas on the E2 this is below the taking lens. Removable hood.

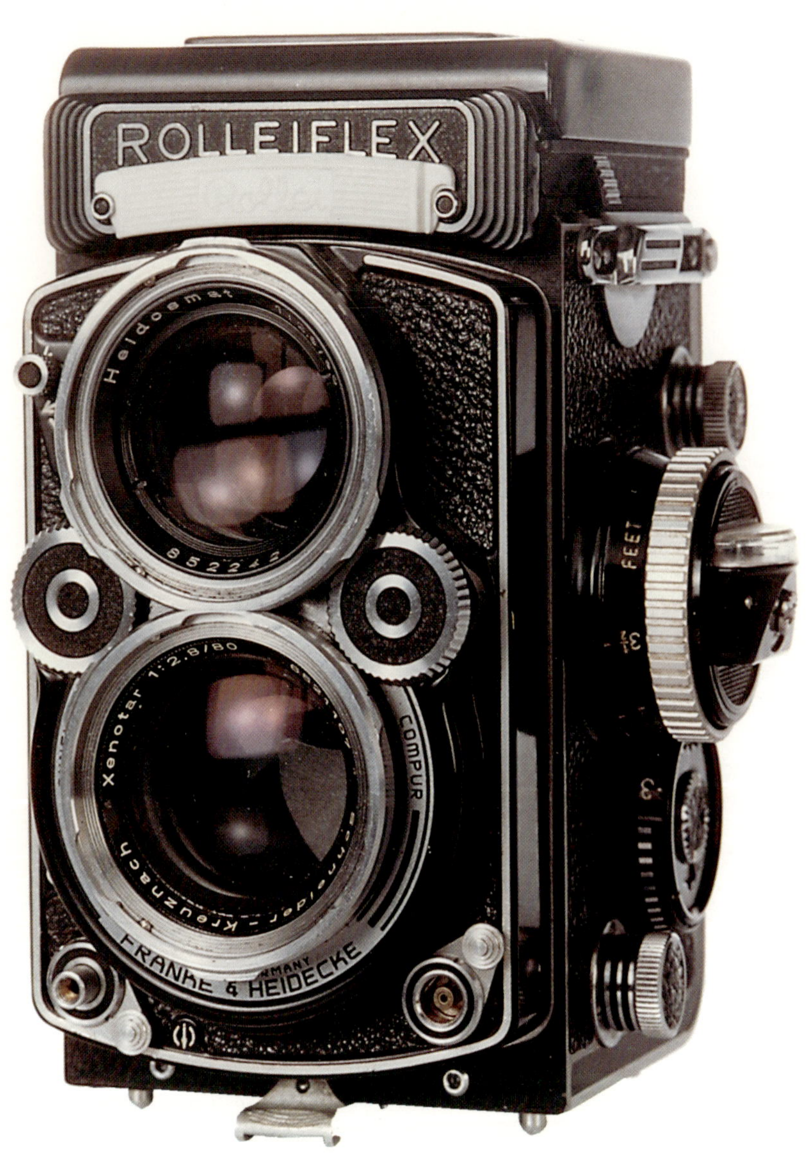

1960 Rolleiflex 2.8F
No. K7F
with meter diffusor

Rolleiflex 2.8F

Factory Model
K7F

Launch Date
02-06-1960

Factory Termination Date
18-09-1981

Serial Numbers
2,400,000 - 2,451,850

Taking Lens
Zeiss Planar f2.8/80mm
Xenotar f2.8/80mm

Finder Lens
Heidosmat
f2.8/80mm

Shutter
Deckel Synchro
Compur MXV

Speeds
1 - 1/500, B

Filter Size
Bayonet III

Film Size
120 or 35mm with Rolleikin

Dimensions
14.8 x 11.2 x 10.4cm

Weight
1250g

Launch Price	Germany	DM880 Planar	USA	$359.00 Planar
		DM820 Xenotar		$349.00 Xenotar
	UK	£147.87 Planar		
		£137.78 Xenotar		

Identification
2.8F precedes serial number. Coupled exposure meter standard but was available without meter. Large filter scale adjustment dial below focusing knob which incorporates film speed setting. This is a feature on all Rolleiflex F Models.

Variations
Focusing distance scales in feet or metres, Planar or Xenotar lens. The camera was available with or without meter but those 'with meter' accounted for 95% of sales. First batch had Rollei logo on hood with gap between the 'R' and the border line. It was possible to install 12 x 24 option. Club Rollei in Jersey can supply meter diffusor cap and replacement meters - see page 176.

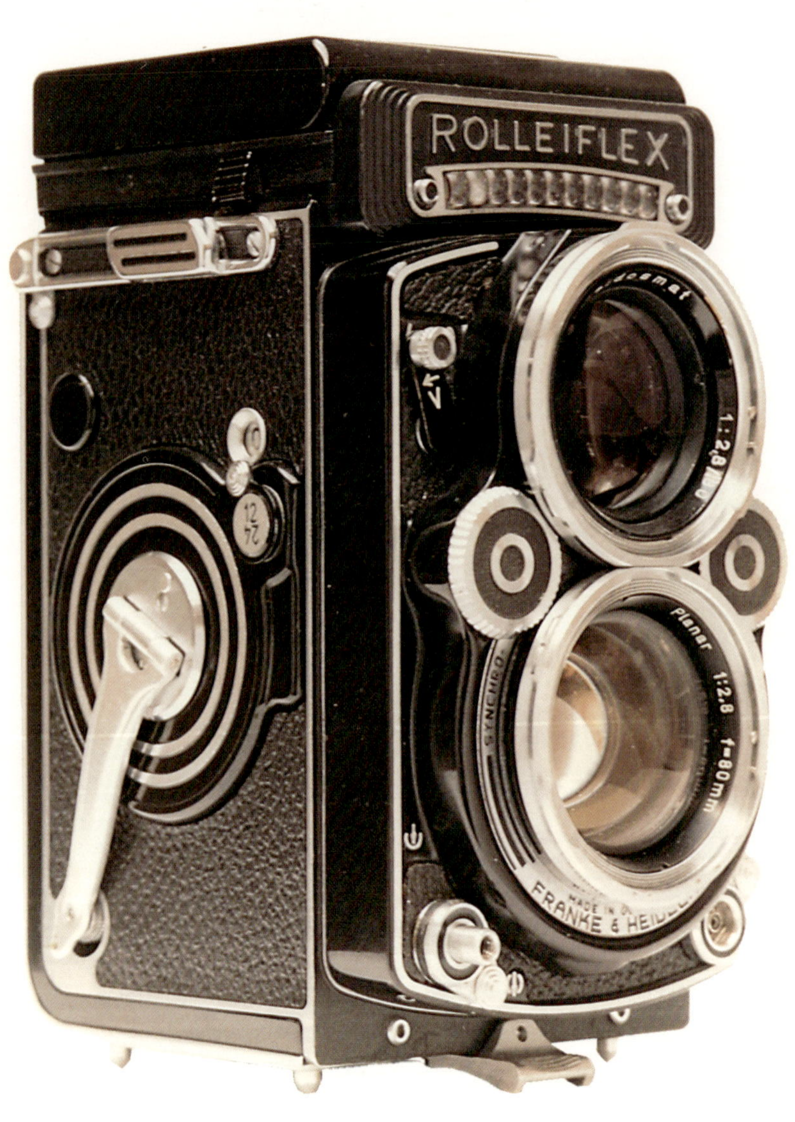

1966 Rolleiflex 2.8F 2/3
No. K7F2/3

Rolleiflex 2.8F 2/3

Factory Model
K7F2/3

Launch Date
00-00-1966

Factory Termination Date
00-00-1976

Serial Numbers
2,451,851 - 2,479,999 (F2-1966)
2,600,000 - 2,799,999 (F3-1969)

Taking Lens
Zeiss Planar f2.8/80mm
Schneider Xenotar f2.8/80mm

Finder Lens
Heidosmat
f2.8/80mm

Shutter
Deckel Synchro
Compur MXV

Speeds
1 - 1/500, B

Filter Size
Bayonet III

Film Size
120 or 35mm with Rolleikin

Dimensions
14.8 x 11.2 x 10.5cm

Weight
1220g

Launch Price Germany DM880 Planar USA $449.50 Planar

UK £174.46 Planar with meter

Identification
Space for 220 film counter option. The half moon metal plate below the scissor strap lug had gone. Distance scale in metres and feet.

Variations
The serial number located below taking lens, with name change to Rollei-Werke Franke & Heidecke followed by serial number.

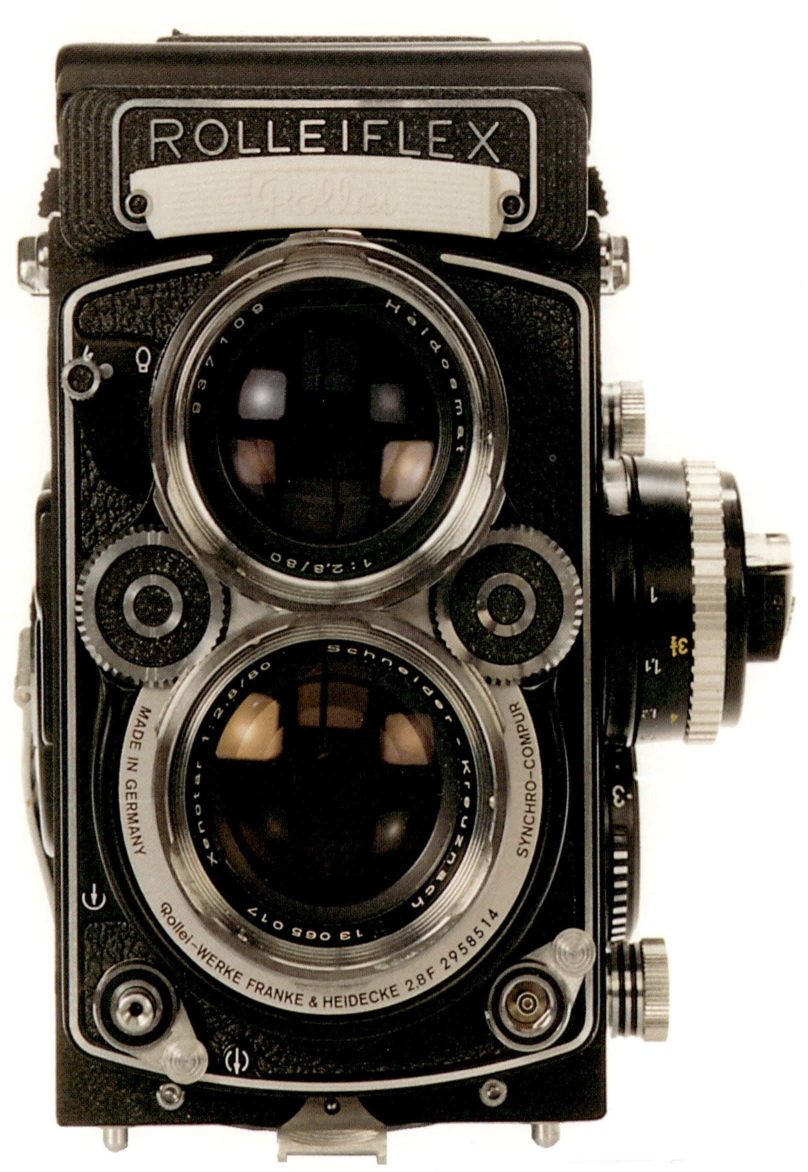

1976 Rolleiflex 2.8F 4
No. K7F4
Note serial number below taking lens

Rolleiflex 2.8F 4

Factory Model
K7F 4

Launch Date
1976

Factory Termination Date
00-10-1980

Serial Numbers
2,900,000 - 2,959,999

Taking Lens
Schneider Xenotar
f2.8/80mm

Finder Lens
Heidosmat
f2.8/80mm

Shutter
Deckel Synchro
Compur MXV

Speeds
1 - 1/500, B

Filter Size
Bayonet III

Film Size
120 or 35mm with Rolleikin

Dimension
14.8 x 11.2 x 10.5cm

Weight
1220g

Launch Price Germany DM1005 USA $912 UK £413.00

Identification

This model only available with Schneider Xenotar lens. Black leather with coarser grain. The last known 2.8F to the Jersey Photographic Museum is No. 2,959,247. Rollei notified all distributors in mid November 1980 that production had finished and no orders could be accepted once existing stock had been sold. The last cameras sold were in December 1980.

Variations

The main variation is the price. In the USA the 1976 price of $912 rose to $967 in 1977, to $1785 in 1980. In the UK the price in 1976 was £413 or, with 220 option, £428.50, but similarly by 1978 the price had risen to £556. In 1980 AV Distributors of the UK sold their last 2.8F in December 1980 to Dixons of Bond Street - the retail price was £560 without VAT.

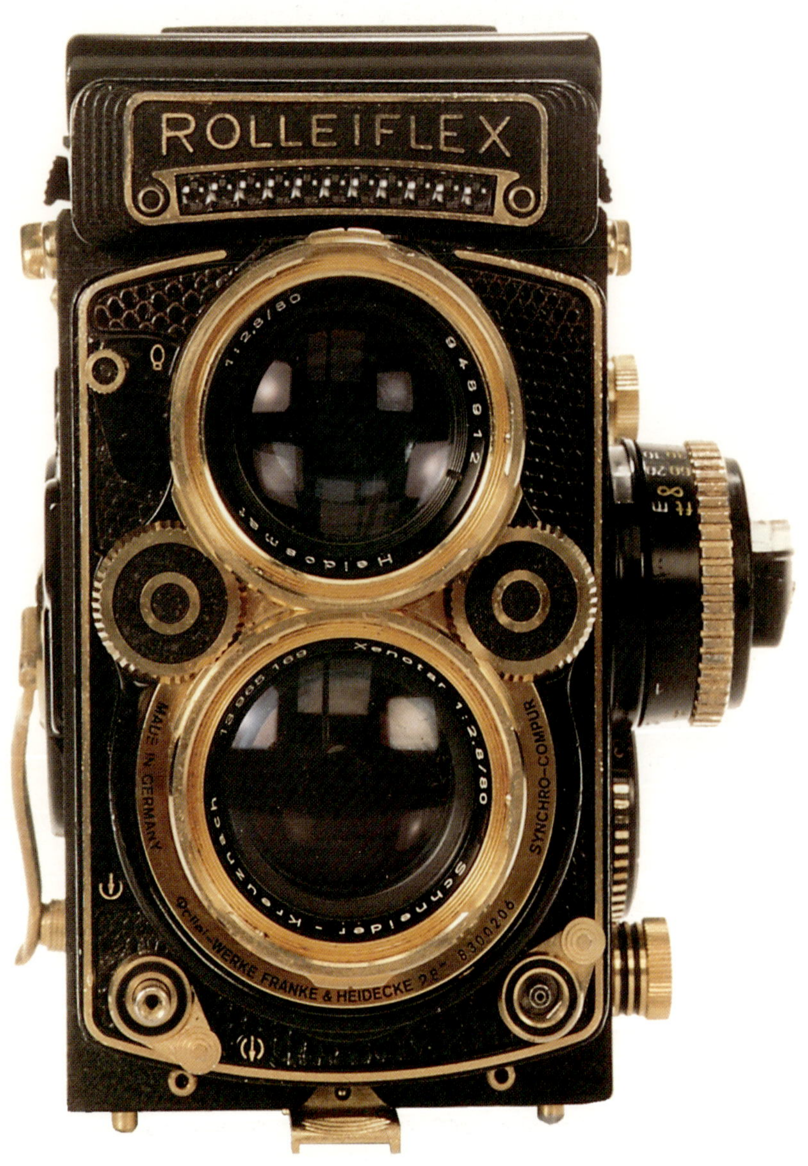

1982 Rolleiflex 2.8F Aurum
No. K7F Aurum

Rolleiflex 2.8F Aurum

Factory Model
K7F Aurum

Launch Date
1982

Factory Termination Date
1984

Serial Numbers

7,570,001 - 7,571,249	1982
8,300,000 - 8,301,499	1983

Taking Lens
Schneider Xenotar
f2.8/80mm

Finder Lens
Heidosmat
f2.8/80mm

Shutter
Deckel Synchro-Compur MXV

Speeds
1 - 1/500, B

Filter Size
Bayonet III

Film Size
120

Dimensions
14.8 x 11.2 x 10.5cm

Weight
1220g

Launch Price Germany DM4000 USA $2700 UK £1750

Identification
23 Carat gold-plated exterior parts, alligator leather, a black red lined wooden case and brown leather scissor strap, also with gold-plated metal parts, made up this package. Although expensive, many society photographers used the Aurum TLR, but many, many more just kept their camera, never used, in a box. So popular was the Aurum that a further 1500 were made.

Variations
There is no difference between the 1982 and 1983 production runs. The original un-numbered prototype had a different logo on the hood and different inscription around the taking lens. This camera was used by Rollei's Managing Director, Norbert Platt, and is in the Jersey Photographic Museum. All Aurum cameras fitted with Xenotar lens. Some cameras, as photo, with black alligator leather but mostly dark brown.

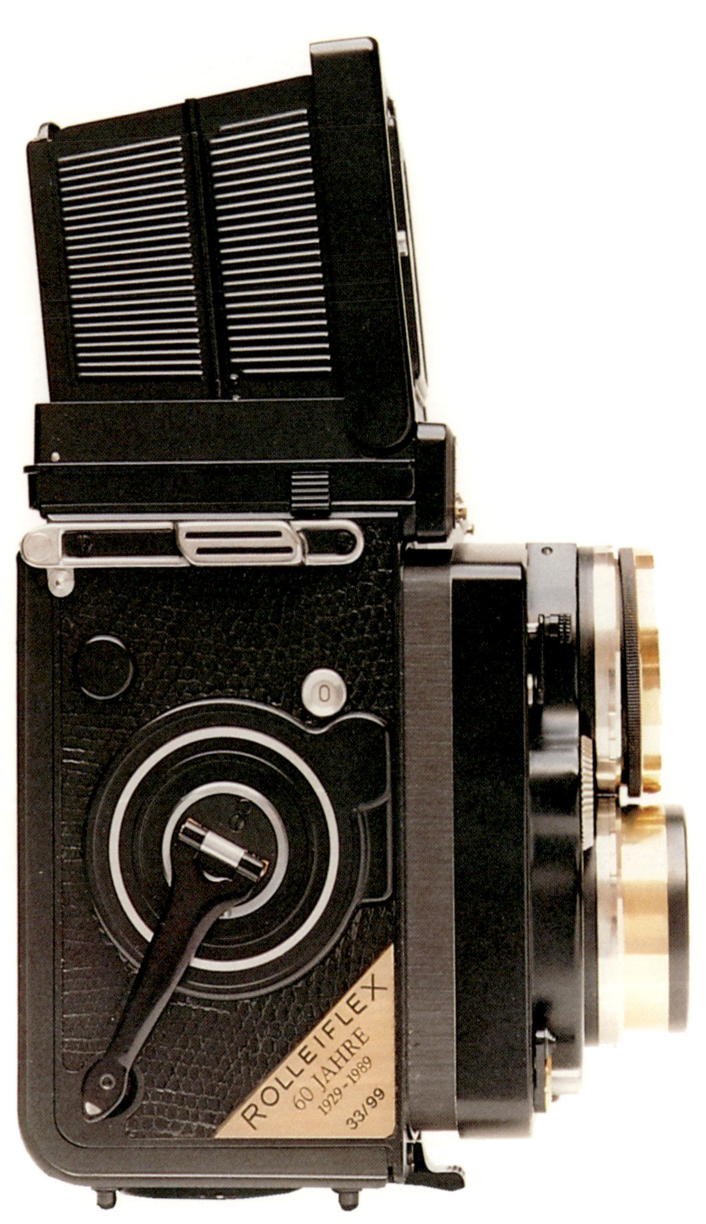

1989 Rolleiflex 2.8F Aurum Platin
No. K7FPA

Rolleiflex 2.8F Platin

Factory Model
K7FP/K7FPA

Launch Date
00-09-1984

Factory Termination Date
00-04-1990

Serial Numbers
2,985,000 - 2,985,499 K7FP(1984)
2,986,500 - 2,986,599 K7FPA (1989)

Taking Lens
Carl Zeiss Planar
f2.8/80mm HFT

Finder Lens
Carl Zeiss Triotar
f2.8/80mm HFT

Shutter
Deckel Synchro
Compur MXV

Speeds
1 - 1/500, B

Filter Size
Bayonet III

Film Size
120

Dimensions
14.8 x 11.2 x 10.5cm

Weight
1225g

Launch Price Germany DM9000 USA $2700.00
UK £4347.00

Identification
Black crocodile leather, Platin treated lens mount presentation case, and Carl Zeiss Planar HFT Lens, to be found on subsequent Rollei TLR cameras. If you have a black 2.8F Rollei with a HFT lens then you own a valuable and collectable 2.8F Platin.

Variations
As a result of an order from the Far East who preferred gold-plating, a small production of exactly 100 cameras was made. These cameras, with gold-plated name, side-plate with camera number and gold-plated close-up lenses were specially made in 1989/90. Code No.K7FPA on the 1989 model.

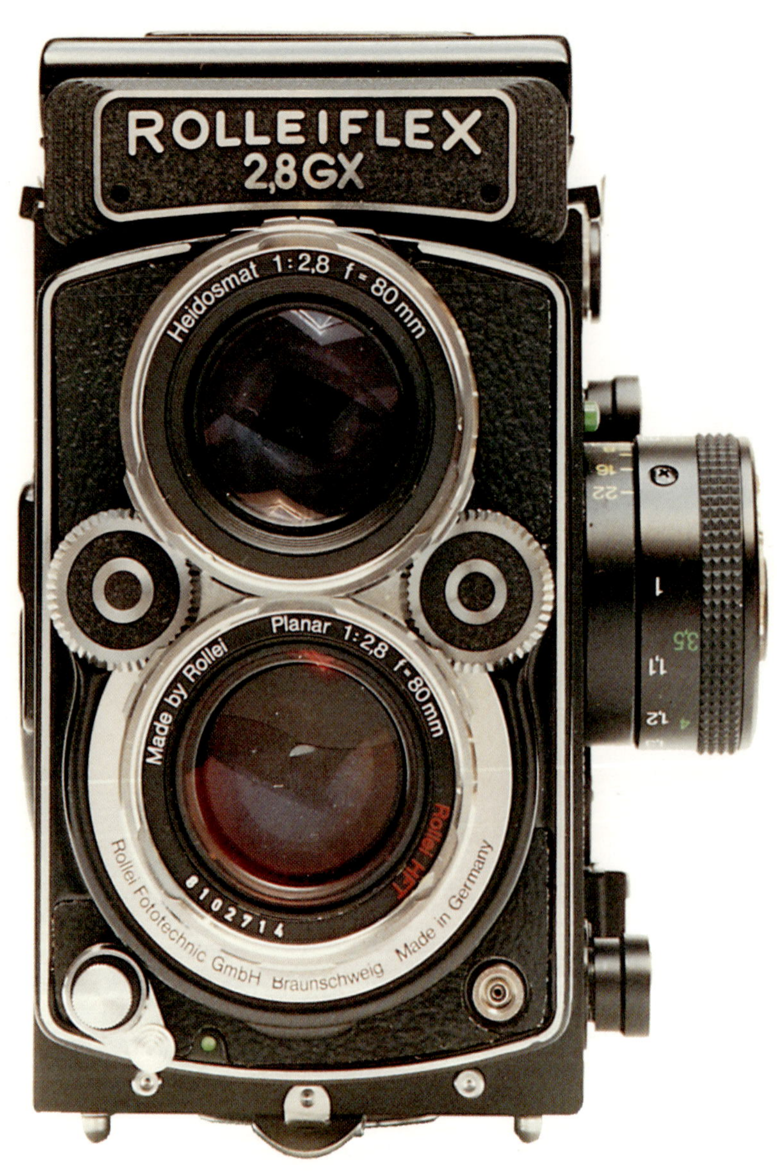

1987 Rolleiflex 2.8GX
No. K7G
First model note sync. socket

Rolleiflex 2.8GX

Factory Model
K7G

Launch Date
00-06-1987

Factory Termination Date
Still in production

Serial Numbers
2,985,500 - Production run not completed

Taking Lens
Rollei Planar HFT
f2.8/80mm

Finder Lens
Heidosmat
f2.8/80mm

Shutter
Deckel Synchro
Compur X

Speeds
1 - 1/500, B

Filter Size
Bayonet III

Film Size
120

Dimensions
14.7 x 10.9 x 10.8cm

Weight
1275g (45oz)

Launch Price	Germany	DM2750	USA	$3000.00
	UK	£1106.30		

Identification
Rollei name on hood, 2.8GX on name plate. No self-timer or bulb flash setting. TTL flash metering, 120 film only, no 35mm provision PX 28 battery is required for the exposure meter with 5 leds indicated in the viewfinder. Flash synchronization as all Rollei TLR's with X to fastest available shutter speed.

Variations
The 2.8GX was announced in January 1987 but deliveries did not commence until July in the domestic market, and in December 1987 in the UK and USA. The price had risen to UK £1299.50 and in Germany DM3000. So far the only variation is a plate on the back, and GmbH deleted after Rollei Fototechnic name on taking lens panel on serial No. after 6,000,000. Later models with redesigned sync. socket.

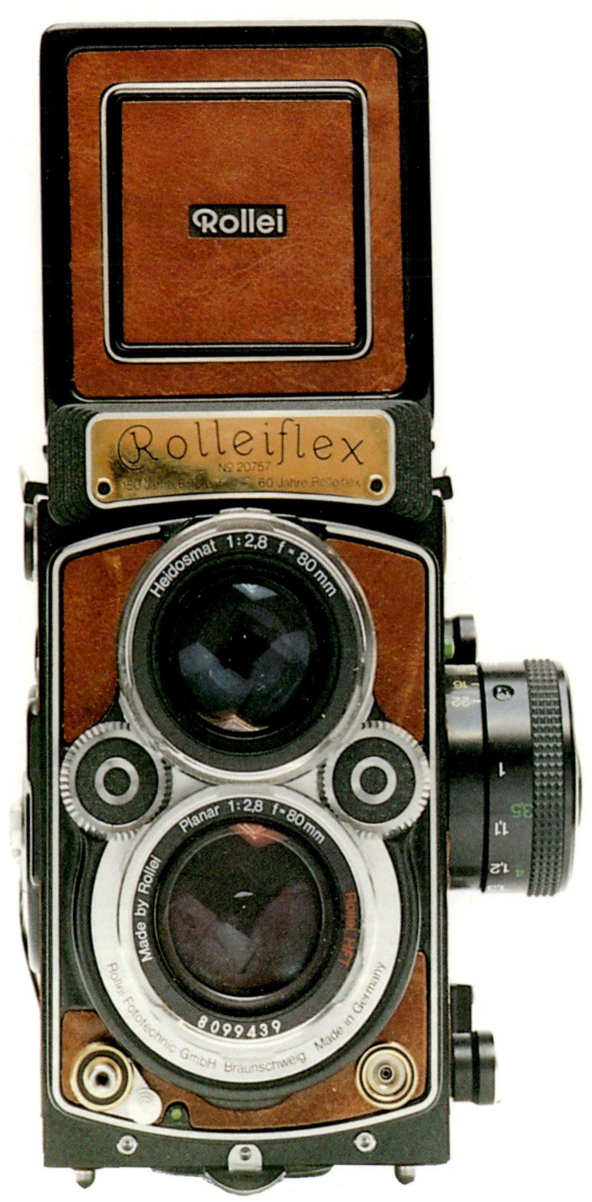

One of several prototypes considered for the 2.8GX in the Jersey Photographic Museum

Rolleiflex 2.8GX Prototypes

Perhaps this is a good place to explain about the current range of Rollei TLR cameras. Basically they are all the same, except for that "cosmetic" name given to anything that has received a little help to brighten up, I suppose, our daily lives. The current range of 2.8GX consist of the standard black 2.8GX which has remained unaltered, except for a small change on the lens panel where GmbH has been omitted and a metal plate on the camera back which is affixed to the film label pocket. Late 1992 saw the introduction of the Grey Helmut Newton Edition of 500 pieces which replaced the 1989 Special Edition camera. Except for the different exterior coloured leathers and paint trim, all these cameras are the same.

Some may well ask why photographers have these Special Editions which are costly and do not perform any better than the standard black 2.8GX. The answer is that these Special Editions do take better shots - why? A photographer using his Special Edition 2.8GX at a wedding, fashion or portrait session will find that his subject, on looking at the camera, will notice that the photographer has something special. Was the camera won in a competition? Or is the camera a special professional model? All this help to inspire confidence in the photographer's subject, also giving the camera user that extra confidence, with the resultant better shots. For landscapes and many other subjects there should be no difference, but for the small additional cost of the special edition you certainly attract admiring glances.

Sadly today the high cost of the Compur shutter, two lenses and being hand built ensures that today's prices for the Rollei 2.8GX are beyond the reach of most photographers. Fortunately, very usable second hand Rollei TLR cameras are easily found at a fraction of today's new prices.

1994 Rolleiflex 2.8GX prices:

Germany DM3999	USA $3250	UK £2113

Helmut Newton Edition:

Germany DM4499	USA $3495	UK £2348.50

NB: German and UK prices include tax; USA prices exclusive of tax.

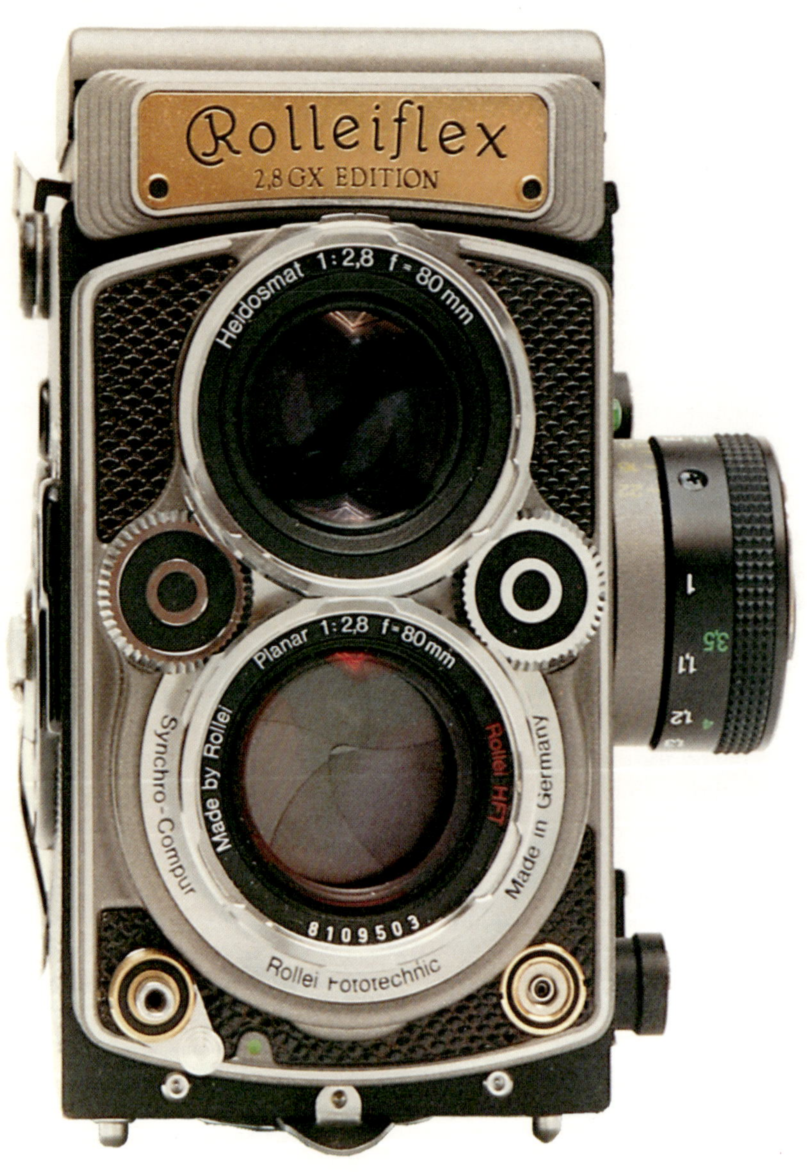

1989 Rolleiflex 2.8GX Edition
_No. K7GE_
As used by the author

Rolleiflex 2.8GX Edition
Helmut Newton Edition

Factory Model
K7GE/K7GHN

Launch Date
Nov. 1989 (Edition)
Sep. 1992 (Newton)

Factory Termination Date
June 1991 (Edition)
Feb. 1993 (Newton)

Serial Numbers
5,010,000 - 5,017,999 (Edition)
6,030,000 - 8,036,999 (Newton)

Taking Lens
Rollei Planar HFT
f2.8/80mm

Finder Lens
Heidosmat
f2.8/80mm

Shutter
Deckel Synchro
Compur X

Speeds
1 - 1/500, B

Filter Size
Bayonet III

Film Size
120

Dimensions
14.7 x 10.9 x 10.8cm

Weight
1275g (45oz)

Launch Price Germany DM3500 USA $3250.00
UK £1495.00

Identification
Edition camera metallic bronze/grey paint to exterior metal, napa leather, gold 1929 style name plate. The camera specification is identical to the 2.8GX, with a total production of 1500. Name on taking lens panel "Synchro-Compur Rollei Fototechnic Made in Germany".

Variations
Helmut Newton Edition, identical to 2.8GX black except grey leather. Helmut Newton signature on plate, back of camera name on taking lens panel - "Rollei Fototechnic" without GmbH as on standard 2.8GX black.

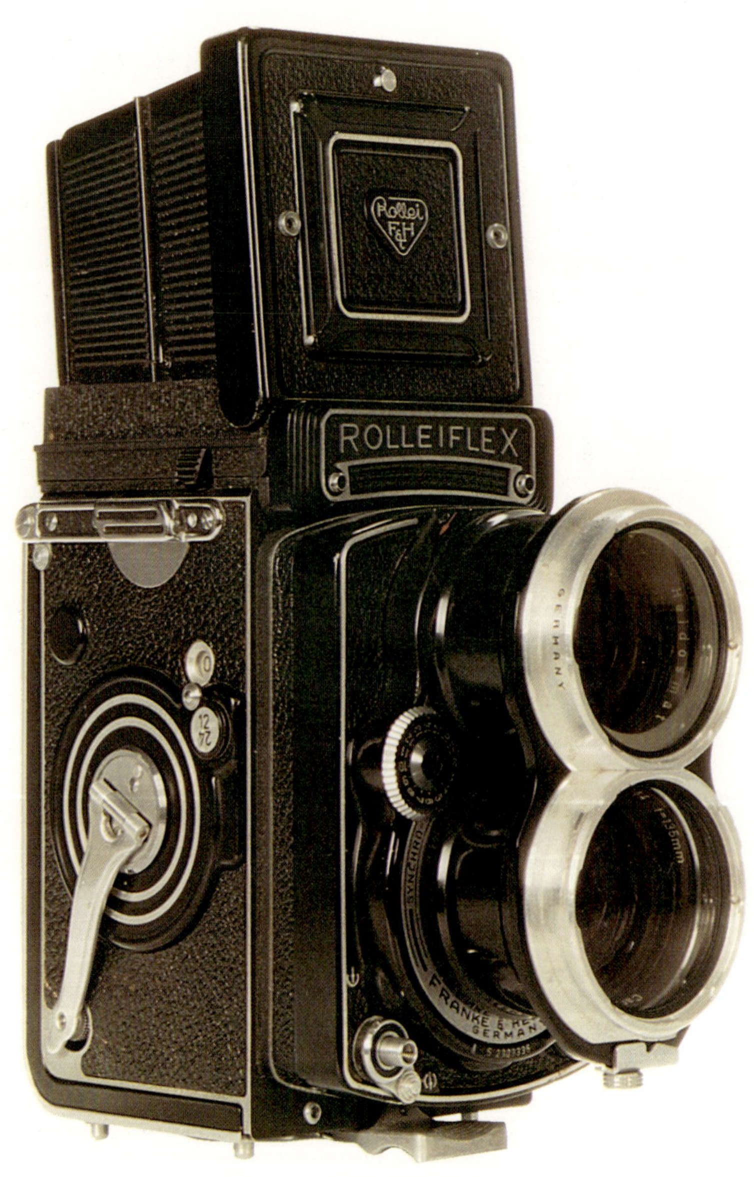

1970 Tele Rolleiflex

with 12/24 (120/220) option and with special close up Rolleinar

Rollei Tele & Wide-Angle TLR

As has been mentioned elsewhere in this book, the perfect camera has not been invented, nevertheless, as far as medium format cameras go, the Rollei TLR which is light and dependable takes a lot of beating. In the 1950's, with Japan's growing camera trade now building TLR cameras with interchangeable lenses, Rollei decided to market in 1959 a Tele TLR with an ideal portrait lens with the Zeiss 135/f4 Sonnar and, unfortunately, with a f4 finder lens. I say 'unfortunately' as this camera would have been a real cracker if only the finder lens could have been f2.8, thus giving portrait photographers a better chance to see whether their subject's eyes were closed. For close up work 2 Rolleinar sets were provided as the two lenses were too close together to allow a standard Bayonet 3 Rolleinar set to be used.

The numbers of Tele cameras sold was modest, but sufficient for another batch to be built in 1970. The difference between the two production runs is negligible, only the Rolleikin counter was deleted and the larger film spool knob reverting to the smaller standard knob as used on the 2.8 or 3.5F.

The Wide-Angle camera, requiring a Bayonet IV filter, with sales of only 4,000, was a disappointment. Although the actual camera cost was pitched at the right level, dealers were reluctant to stock an assortment of Bayonet IV filters which each cost 3% of the camera price.

Today both cameras are much sought after by both collectors and users alike, and therefore command premium prices.

Tele & Wide-Angle Rolleiflex:

Serial Nos.	Model Type	Factory No.	Year	Page
2,300,000 - 2,304,999	Tele	K75	1959	155
2,305,000 - 2,308,377	Tele	K75	1970	155
2,490,000 - 2,493,999	Wide-Angle	K7W	1961	157

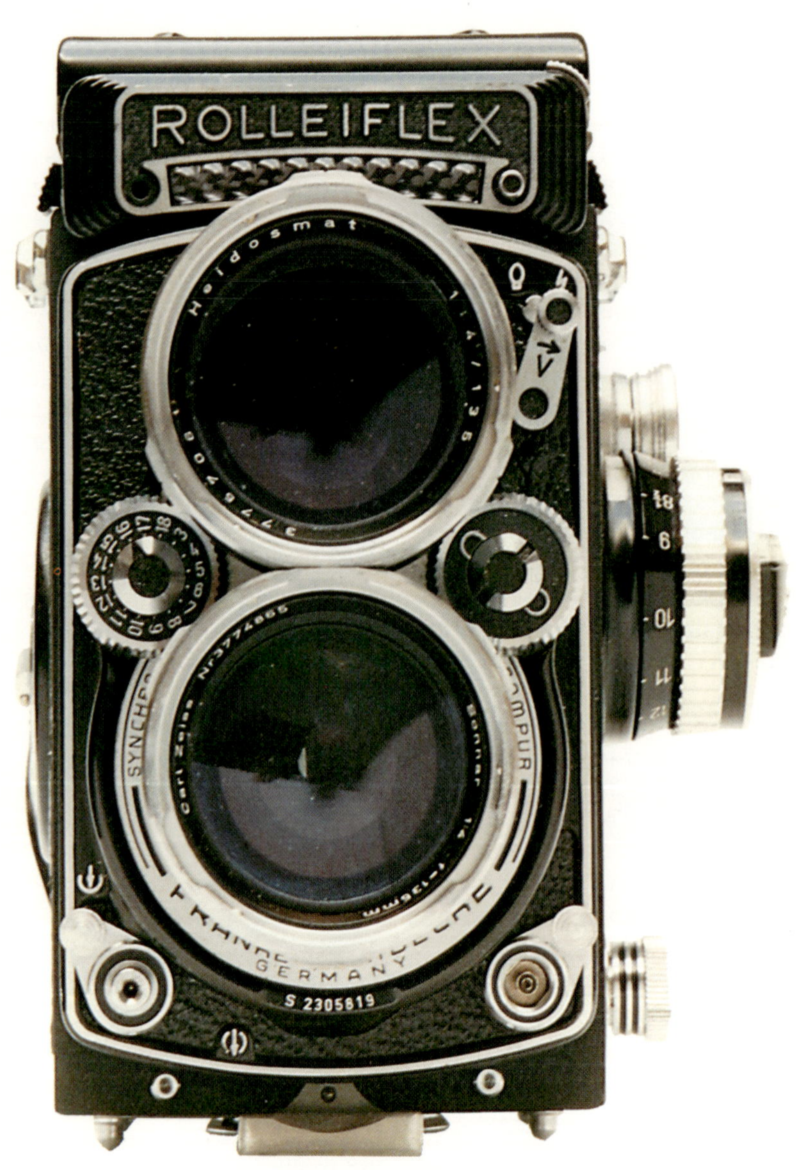

1959 Tele Rolleiflex
No. K75
with 135mm f4 Sonnar lens

Tele Rolleiflex

Factory Model
K75

Launch Date
22-05-1959

Factory Termination Date
08-11-1974

Serial Numbers
S2,300,000 - S2,304,999 1959
S2,305,000 - S2,308,377 1970

Taking Lens
Zeiss Sonnar
f4/135mm

Finder Lens
Heidosmat
f4/135mm

Shutter
Deckel Synchro-Compur MXV

Speeds
1 - 1/500, B

Filter Size
Bayonet III

Film Size
120 or 35mm with Rolleikin

Dimensions
14.8 x 10.5 x 14cm

Weight
1535g (54oz)

Launch Price Germany DM1071 USA $659.00 UK £186.31

Identification

Larger protruding fixed lens 135mm not found on any other Rollei TLR. As with other 1959 Rollei's the tele had removable hood, optically flat glass provision to keep film flat and, except for lens, was similar to the Rollei f2.8E. Serial number was preceded by S (for Sonnar) and located below taking lens.

Variations

New type sports finder. Prior to 2,304,999 the camera was supplied with 35mm counter. The1970 model omitted this. A meter type T could be fitted; factory code for exposure metered cameras K8S. A special close up accessory is required to focus closer than 2.8 metres (8ft 6 inches). The 1970 model with smaller film spool pull out knobs same as 2.8F. The 12/24 option could be fitted on all Tele cameras from No. 2,304,999.

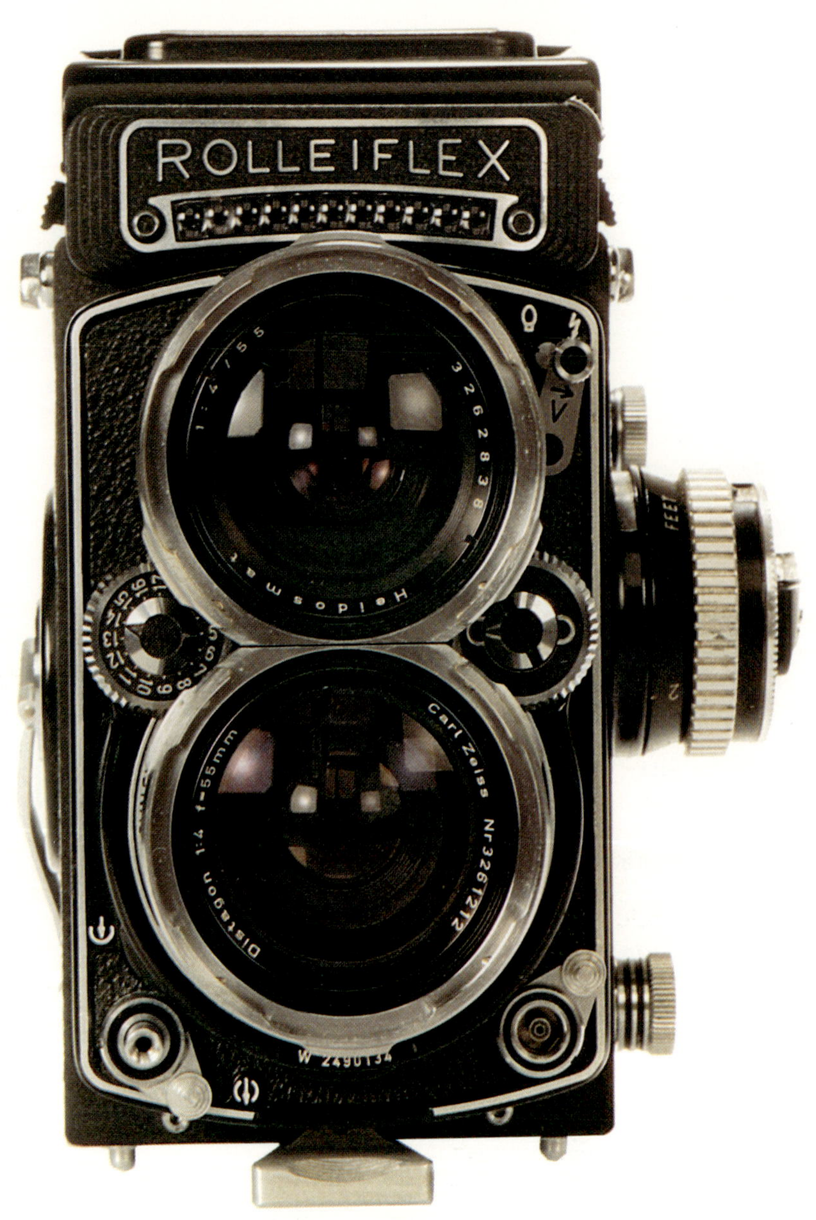

1961 Wide-Angle Rolleiflex
No. K7W
Note serial number below taking lens

Wide-Angle Rolleiflex

Factory Model
K7W

Launch Date
10-04-1961

Factory Termination Date
00-07-1967

Serial Numbers
2,490,000 - 2,493,999

Taking Lens
Carl Zeiss Distagon
f4/55mm

Finder Lens
Heidosmat
f4/55m

Shutter
Deckel Synchro
Compur MXV

Speeds
1 - 1/500, B

Filter Size
Bayonet IV

Film Size
120 or 35mm with Rolleikin

Dimensions
15.2 x 11.3 x 12.8cm

Weight
1360g (53oz)

Launch Price Germany DM975 USA $400.00 UK £220.42

Identification
This was the only Rollei TLR with a wide-angle 55mm lens. Rollei did try to design a camera on a f2.8 E2 body that would take interchangeable lenses similar to the Mamiya concept, they decided it was not possible and the fixed lensed Tele and Wide-Angle was made. The wide-angle lens was not easily installed in the f2.8 E2, but many wide-angle Rollei TLR cameras offered for sale have been converted Tele or f2.8 E2s.

Variations
During the seven year life of this camera poor sales accounted for the small numbers made. In 1963, to remove stocks, a price reduction stimulated demand. By 1964 the price reverted back to the launch price, and by 1966 had increased by 20%. Variations included an exposure meter option with provision for optical flat glass from 1964.

The Rollei Magics

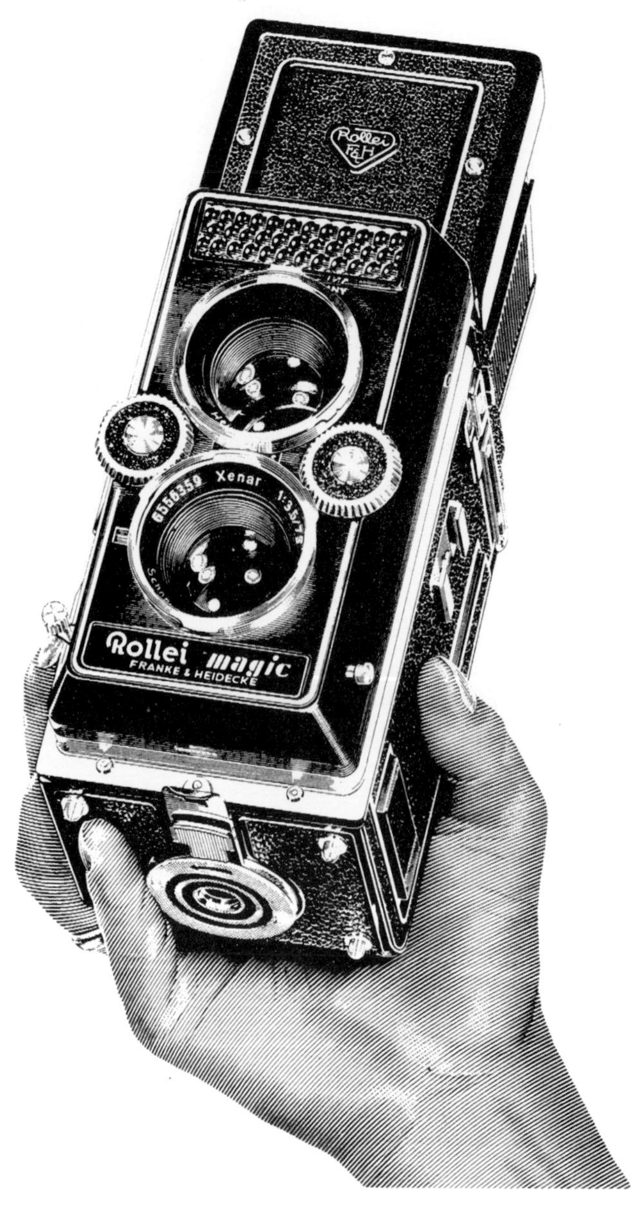

The Rollei Magic TLR

Many, oh so many, Rollei TLR enthusiasts were outraged that their preserve, the traditional, practical and the best engineered camera from Germany, should be joined by an automated camera whose build quality they considered debased the Rollei name. The fact that the Rollei Magic attracted countless more Rollei customers who in turn later bought the traditional camera did not matter.

The Magic, although not a runaway commercial success some may say, did at least sell over 32,000 cameras and, some 35 years since the camera went on sale, many are still in use today. However, many who bought the camera when the Magic was the 'flavour of the month' soon discarded this 6 x 6 marvel for the smaller 35mm SLR camera and so clean, virtually mint, examples of the Mark I version are not too difficult to find at the same price as today's compact 35mm camera - in the UK £175/£200.

The camera is easily damaged if badly treated by those who do not know how the camera functions. Do check before purchase: Rollei Magics are difficult to repair. Rollei Magics are not for the serious amateur or professional so your collection should include a good clean example.

Rollei Magic TLR:

Serial No.	Model Type	Factory No.	Year	Page
2,500,000 - 2,534,999	Magic	K9	1960	161
2,535,000 - 2,547,597	Magic II	K9 II	1962	163

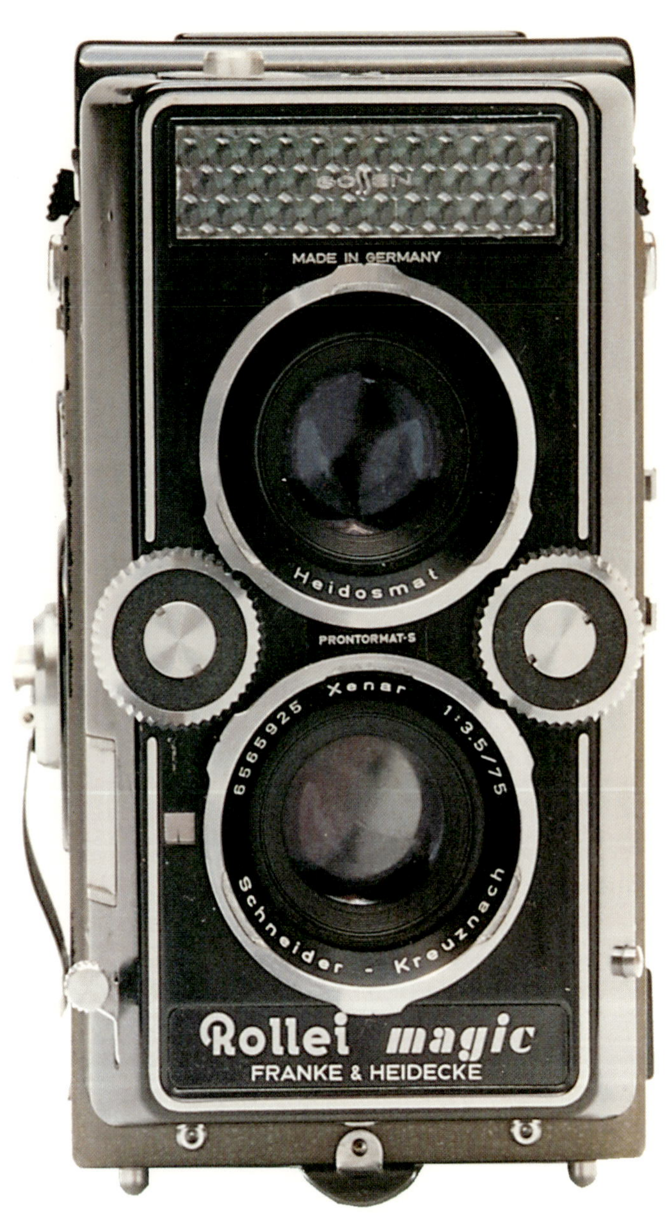

1960 Rollei Magic I
No. K9

Rollei Magic I

Factory Model
K9

Launch Date
12-10-1960

Factory Termination Date
14-03-1962

Serial Numbers
2,500,000 - 2,534,999

Taking Lens
Schneider Xenar
f3.5/75mm

Finder Lens
Heidosmat
f3.5/75mm

Shutter
Deckel Prontormat S

Speeds
B, 1/30 - 1/300

Filter Size
Bayonet II

Film Size
120

Dimensions
14.5 x 8.8 x 10.6cm

Weight
980g (42oz)

Launch Price Germany DM435 USA $170.00 UK £124.50

Identification

Nameplate Rollei Magic below taking lens. This is a simpler camera than the Rollei Magic II. Instruction book essential. Prone to meter failure which costs more to repair than the mint second hand price. Large Gossen Selinium cells above finder lens. Unusual flat film holder accounts for absence of normal film holder knobs.

Variations

No variations except for MkII version (as shown on next page). Interestingly, unrepairable cameras have a value for the removable new type hood. A camera not for the user of nervous disposition who may wonder if the manual meter is working. Novices enjoy the fully automatic camera and obtain photographs equally as good as with the Rolleicord or Rolleiflex T. A must for the collector. Serial number located beneath lens panel adjoining back opening catch.

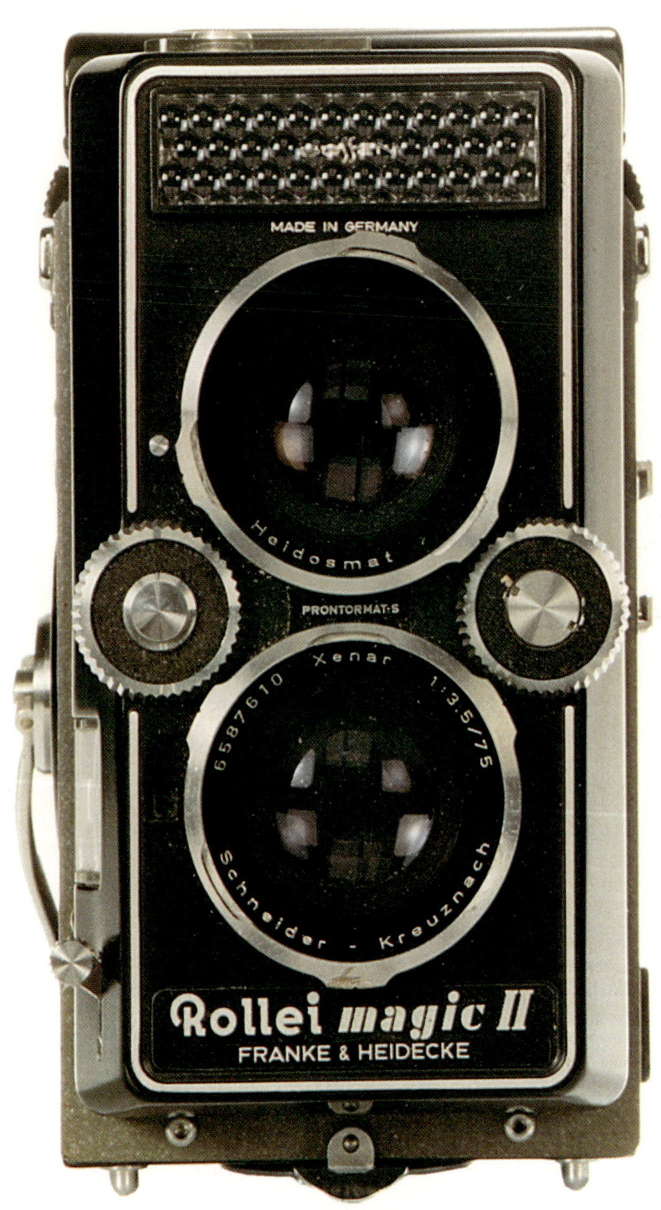

1962 Rollei Magic II
No. K9 II

Rollei Magic II

Factory Model
K9 II

Launch Date
14-03-1962

Factory Termination Date
30-07-1968

Serial Numbers
2,535,000 - 2,547,597

Taking Lens
Schneider
f3.5/75mm

Finder Lens
Heidosmat
f3.5/75mm

Shutter
Deckel Prontormat S

Speeds
B, 1/30 - 1/500

Filter Size
Bayonet II

Film Size
120

Dimensions
14.7 x 8.8 x 10.6cm

Weight
990g

Launch Date Germany DM498 USA $185 UK £147.25

Identification

Nameplate below taking lens. Serial number located beneath lens panel adjoining camera back catch. Rollei Magic II both manual and automatic operation. Top shutter speed 1/500th.

Variations

The Rollei Magic II is the more desirable users' camera with manual setting option. Mask sets as used in the Rolleicord are available giving 16 exposures on both Magic I and II. The collector will pay more for the Magic II with a production run of only 13,597. The Rollei Magic requires a specially dedicated strap, otherwise it is almost impossible to attach a strap.

Please Note

It is not possible to include every prototype, those special cameras whose leather trim was of different colour to the standard black or grey that was so altered for a particular presentation or to attract attention at an exhibition - the number of pages does not allow the space. For the same reason cameras that were not available for sale to the general public have not been included unless they might appear on the second hand market, as is the case with the special Rolleicord cameras listed on pages 65 and 67.

The Jersey Photographic Museum has many examples of one off prototypes of special cameras. Should you have such a camera do let us know giving camera and lens serial numbers together with a photo and we shall do our best to tell you something about your camera.

Rolleicord serial numbers: Why have we listed lens numbers when the camera serial number can be found on opening the camera back and the number is located on the casting over the bottom take up spool with numbers prefixed by "0"? Some dealers, and of course should there be a film in the camera, may not welcome the back being opened to enable you to check the camera serial number. On visiting Zeiss Jena last year they gave us a list of lens numbers and dates from Jan 1, 1928 to 1939. Unfortunately lenses were not placed in the cameras in any order, but likewise the camera numbered body numbers are also unreliable as it is said they carried the invoice number in the early days to give the impression that business was booming. Invoice numbers, which also included those for stereo cameras, filters, and accessories, would give the impression that more cameras were being sold than was the case.

We decided that with the Zeiss lens dates becoming available this was an easier method to recognise a camera without having to open the back and seek a number that did not really give any more precise information. Franke & Heidecke accounted for 80% of Zeiss camera lens production. Zeiss were very meticulous on their numbering, so if your camera lens number was 920,000 (see page 5) you would know that the lens was manufactured in 1929 and the camera was built in 1929/1930, at any rate the camera's age could not be 1928.

INDEX

Serial Nos.	Camera Type	Date	Page No.
Rolleiflex:			
125,000 - 145,100	Baby 4x4	1931-1932	11
150,000 - 154,999	Baby 4x4	1933-1934	13
155,000 - 524,999	Baby 4x4	1934-1938	15
622,000 - 734,999	Baby 4x4 (430)	1938-1943	17
850,000 - 850,999	Baby 4x4 (440)	1938-1943	17
2,000,001 - 2,064,999	Baby 4x4	1957-1961	19
2,065,000 - 2,069,999	Baby 4x4	1963-1963	21
Rolleicord:			
1,460,000 - 1,759,000*	Art Deco	1933-1936	27
1,590,000 - 1,759,999*	Model I	1934-1936	29
1,760,000 - 1,947,000*	Model Ia	1936-1937	31
1,758,000 - 1,973,999*	Model II	1936-1937	33
1,945,000 - 2,183,000*	Model Ia Type 4.5	1937-1938	35
1,966,000 - 2,124,000*	Model IIa F3.5	1937-1938	37
611,000 - 1,042,999**	Model Ia Type 3	1938-1945	39
612,000 - 858,999**	Model IIb	1938-1939	41
859,000 - 1,006,999**	Model IIc	1939-1949	43
1,007,000 - 1,134,999**	Model IId	1949-1950	45
1,135,000 - 1,135,999**	Model IIe	1949-1950	47
1,137,000 - 1,344,050**	Model III	1950-1953	49
1,344,051 - 1,390,999**	Model IV	1952-1954	51
1,500,000 - 1,583,999**	Model V	1954-1957	53
1,584,000 - 1,599,999**	Model Va Type 1	1957-1958	55
1,900,000 - 1,943,999**	Model Va Type 2	1958-1961	57
2,600,000 - 2,649,999**	Model Vb Type 1	1962-1970	59
2,650,000 - 2,665,999**	Model Vb Type 2	1970-1971	61
2,666,000 - 2,677,498**	Model Vb Type 3	1971-1976	63
2,610,000 - 2,610,999	Model K3 Vba	1962-1966	65
2,632,000 - 2,632,999	Model K3 Vba	1968-1972	65
2,611,000 - 2,611,499	Model K3 Vbb	1962-1963	65

* Serial No. located on Taking Lens

** Serial No. located on Name Plate

Serial Nos.	Camera Type	Date	Page No.
Original Rolleiflex:			
1 - 199,999	Original 6x6	1928-1932	71
200,000 - 567,000	Standard 620/621	1932-1935/38	73
200,000 - 567,550	Standard 622	1934-1938	75
568,516 - 805,000	Automat Model 1	1937-1939	77
3.5f Rolleiflex:			
805,000 - 1,050,000	Automat Model 2	1939-1945	83
805,000 - 927,999	New Standard	1939-1941	85
1,050,000 - 1,099,999	Automat Model 3	1945-1949	87
1,000,000 - 1,168,000	Automat Model 'X'	1949-1951	89
1,200,000 - 1,427,999	Automat Model	1951-1954	91
1,428,001 - 1,479,999	3.5 MX-EVS	1954-1956	93
1,479,000 - 1,739,999	" "	" "	"
1,740,000 - 1,787,849	3.5E (with lightmeter)	1956-1959	95
1,850,000 - 1,868,442	3.5E(without ")	1956-1959	95
1,870,000 - 1,872,010	3.5E2 (K4C2)	1959-1961	97
2,480,000 - 2,482,999	3.5E2 (K4C3)	1960-1962	97
2,380,000 - 2,385,034	3.5E3	1961-1965	99
2,100,000 - 2,199,999	T1	1958-1966	101
2,220,000 - 2,313,999	T2	1966-1971	103
2,314,000 - 2,320,298	T3	1971-1976	105
2,200,000 - 2,219,999	3.5F Model 1	1958-1960	107
2,230,000 - 2,241,500	3.5F Model 2	1960-1960	109
2,250,000 - 2,299,999	3.5F Model 3	1960-1964	111
2,800,000 - 2,844,999	3.5F Model 4	1965-1976	113
2,845,000 - 2,857,149	3.5F Model 5	1979-1979	115
3,555,000 - 3,559,999	" " "	" "	"
2.8f Rolleiflex:			
1,101,000 - 1,114,999	2.8A Type 1	1949-1951	121
1,115,000 - 1,139,999	" " "	" "	"
1,154,000 - 1,163,999	2.8A Type 2	1951-1951	123
1,201,000 - 1,201,999	" " "	" "	"
1,204,000 - 1,259,999	2.8B	1952-1953	125
1,260,000 - 1,457,405	2.8C	1952-1955	127
1,600,000 - 1,620,100	2.8D	1955-1956	129
1,621,000 - 1,664,999	2.8E	1956-1959	131
2,350,000 - 2,356,999	2.8E Type 2	1959-1960	133
2,360,000 - 2,362,024	2.8E Type 3	1962-1965	135

Serial Nos.	Camera Type	Date	Page No.
2.8f Rolleiflex Cont'd:			
2,400,000 - 2,451,850	2.8F	1960-1981	137
2,451,851 - 2,479,999	2.8F Type 2	1966-1976	139
2,600,000 - 2,799,999	2.8F Type 3	1969-1976	139
2,900,000 - 2,959,999	2.8F Type 4	1976-1980	141
7,570,001 - 7,571,249	2.8F Aurum	1982	143
8,300,000 - 8,301,499	" "	1983	"
2,985,000 - 2,985,499	2.8F Platin	1984-1990	145
2,986,500 - 2,986,599	2.8F Aurum Platin	1989-1990	"
2,985,500 -	2.8GX	1987-	147
5,010,000 - 5,017,999	2.8GX Edition	1989-1991	151
6,030,000 - 8,036,999	2.8GX H. Newton	1992-1993	"
Tele & Wide-Angle Rolleiflex:			
2,300,000 - 2,304,999	Tele	1959-1974	155
2,305,000 - 2,308,377	"	1970-1974	"
2,490,000 - 2,493,999	Wide-Angle	1961-1967	157
Rollei Magics:			
2,500,000 - 2,534,999	Magic I	1960-1962	161
2,535,000 - 2,547,597	Magic II	1962-1968	163

Jargon Buster

Accessory Holder: Studs on hood to hold Rolleikin masks.

Adapter: Two types of adapter are used for Rollei TLR: (a) Rolleikin to enable 35mm film to be used; (b) for using plates.

Adjustable Pressure Plate: Located inside of camera back, is used for different formats i.e. 35mm.

Aperture: Lens aperture.

Art Deco: Late twenties fashionable style.

Automat: The name given to automatic wind on, shutter cocking.

Bayonet: Rollei used a Bayonet fitting for filters similar to the Bayonet used on SLR camera lenses for fitting into camera rather than a screw thread. Bayonet I for Baby, Cords, Magics and early 3.5F cameras, Bayonet II for later 3.5F cameras, Bayonet III for Tele and 2.8F, Bayonet IV for Wide-Angle, and Bayonet VI for SLR.

Cap: Lens cap, covers and protects lens.

Crank/Cranking: The famous Rollei lever or knob for advancing the film.

Cable Release Socket: This allowed the use of a cable of various lengths to release shutter.

Critical Eye-Level Focusing: Allows the photographer to focus on the ground glass screen through a magnifying glass when holding the camera at eye-level.

Delayed Action: For use when including the photographer

within the shot, or often used by nervous unsteady hands to avoid camera shake with the camera on a tripod.

Etched Nameplate: Acid was used on early cameras to engrave the nameplate before cast iron plates were used.

EVS: Exposure value system. Hand held or camera light meters with EVS scale could be set on the camera thus controlling both aperture and shutter in synchronization.

Eye-Level Finder: Or, as originally known, Sports Level Finder, consists of the hood front flap pressed down allowing the camera to be used at eye-level looking through the small hole on the hood.

Feeler Mechanism: Found on Rolleiflex whereby the film on loading is passed under a "feeler" roller. On closing the camera back, wind on the film, the feeler roller will trip when the additional thickness of the film and backing paper pass under the roller, thus setting film counter and eliminating the need for the red window.

Ground Glass Screen: The screen used for focusing.

Knob: It is sometimes difficult to describe some parts of the Rolleiflex i.e. knob for focusing, winding on film, shutter release, or, in the case of the Rolleiflex T Model I, whereby the aperture and shutter speed levers had a "black knob".

Hood: The metal surrounding the focusing screen to shade from extraneous light which also holds the magnifier.

Masks: Used to show area on screen for different

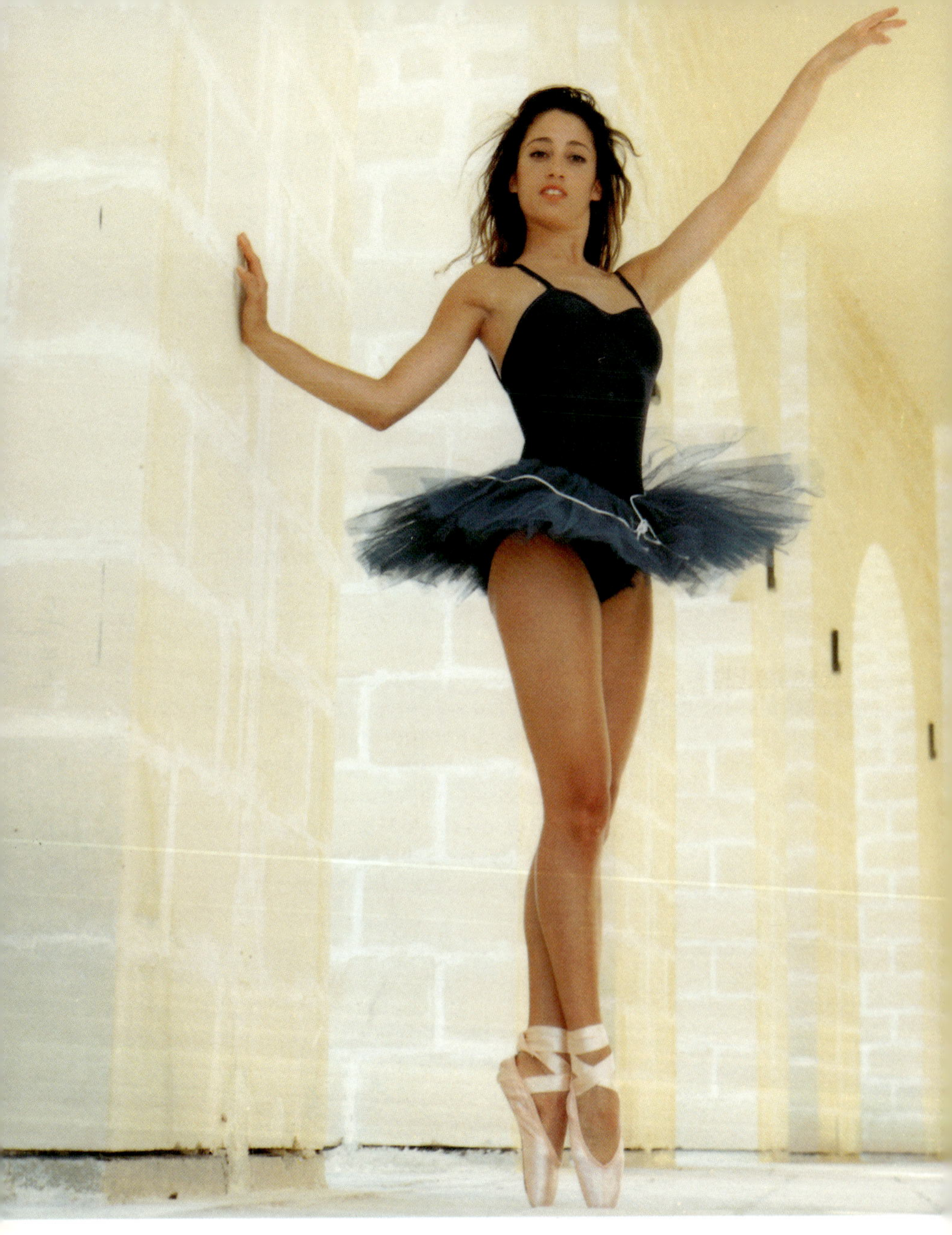

Malta 1993 - Rolleiflex 2.8GX Edition - Ian Parker

Cecil Beaton, Baron, Dorothy Wilding, David Bailey, Thomas Moore, Robert Doisneau, Patrick Lichfield . . . just some of the many photographers, past and present, who have earnt their daily bread with a Rolleiflex.

formats, i.e. 35mm, also for blanking off film chamber inside camera.

Optically Flat Glass: An expensive piece of glass which fitted inside the film chamber to ensure that with the pressure plate pressing on the film back the film remained dead flat.

Peephole: Found above finder lens enabling viewing of aperture and shutter settings.

Plate Back: A special back replaces normal back for using single film or glass plates.

Pressure Plate: Fitted on camera back to hold film flat. On some cameras adjustable for different formats, i.e. 35mm, 6 x 4.5cm.

Pressure Plate Release Pin: A small pin located between the film channel and the outer body, this pin releases the pressure plate while the film is advanced.

Rim-Set: Compur Rim Set shutter introduced in 1928 whereby you set aperture and shutter by small levers on rim.

Rolleikin: 35mm conversion kit available for most Rollei TLR cameras.

Rolleinar: Used for close up and macro photography. Available in Bayonet size I, II, and III. No.I for focusing from 39½ down to 17¾ inches (approx. 1 metre to ½ metre); No.II from 19¾ to 12 1/8 inches (approx. ½ metre to 30cms.); and No.III focusing down to 8 inches (approx. 20cm.).

Synchronization: M setting for flash exposures from 1/50 to 1/500 with flash bulbs. X setting for today's speedlight or electronic flash guns at any speed. Early Rollei with the picture of a bulb for use with PF type bulbs at 1/25th of a second.

Club Rollei

More than a Club:

Magazine Quarterly, Buy and Sale Advertisements free, problems solved where possible by staff and members. Articles on collecting, using, and all about Rollei today and yesterday. Annual meetings in London and Jersey.

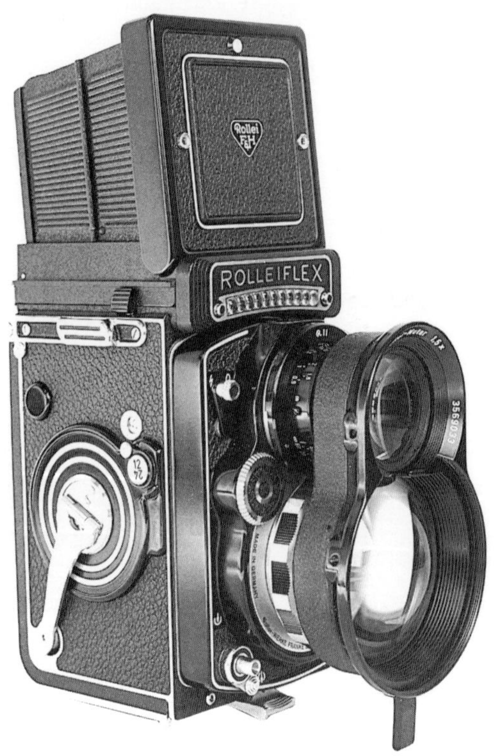

Rolleiflex 3.5F

120/220 with Mutar 1.5X Tele converter from the collection of Terry Sheehy, 39 Beechwood Ave., Orpington, Kent, BR6 7EZ, England.

Terry can provide Rollei reprints on articles, instructions etc. Information free but contributions towards postage appreciated.

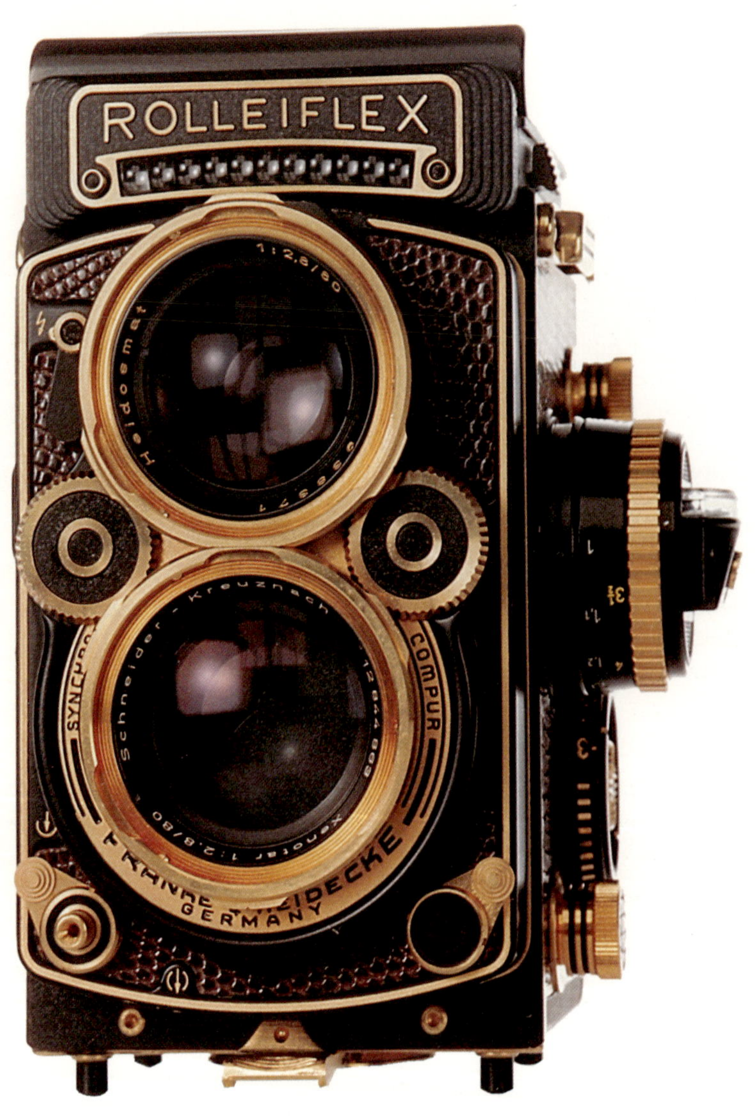

**Once it was every photographers' dream,
professional or amateur,
to own a Rollei TLR**

1981 Rolleiflex 2.8F
Special Presentation Model

Rollei Second-Hand Prices

Second-hand average prices 1994 for excellent, but not mint, Rollei TLR:

Year	Model	Page Nos.	UK	Germany	USA
1931/33	4x4 Baby	9/11/13	£150	DM650	$275
1934/38	4x4 Baby	15/17	£225	DM700	$350
1957	4x4 Grey	19	£175	DM550	$325
1963	4x4 Black	21	£800	DM1250	$1250
1933	Cord Art Deco	27	£200	DM475	$325
1934	Cord Model I	29	£100	DM300	$125
1936/39	Various Cords	31/41	£80	DM250	$125
1949/50	Cord II	43/45	£100	DM275	$135
1949	Cord IIe Xenar	47	£350	DM1250	$500
1950/58	Cord III/Va	49/57	£150	DM275	$350
1962	Cord Vb	59/63	£150/200	DM600	$325
1928/34	Early Flex	71/77	£125	DM275	$250
1937/51	Automat	79/91	£150	DM450/500	$350
1954	Flex EVS	93/99	£200	DM650	$400
1958	Flex T 1 & 2	101/103	£275	DM800	$350
1971	Flex T 3	105	£375	DM1200	$600
1958	Flex 3.5F	107/113	£400	DM1350	$550
1979	Flex 3.5F 5	115	£600	DM1550	$850
1949/51	2.8A	121/123	£275	DM1250	$400
1952	2.8B	125	£450	DM1500	$500
1952/59	2.8C, D & E	127/133	£350	DM1100	$400
1962	2.8E 3	135	£850	DM1750	$600
1960/66	2.8F	137/139	£650	DM1500	$950
1976	2.8F 4	141	£800	DM2000	$1200
1959	Tele	155	£1250	DM2500	$1250
1961	Wide-Angle	157	£1750	DM4500	$2750
1960	Magic I	161	£175	DM475	$300
1962	Magic II	163	£250	DM600	$350

Club Rollei Sales

With each issue of the Club magazine there is a comprehensive list of items to fit your Rollei T.L.R. cameras.

Examples currently available New & Used

Subject to availability

Improve your viewing with a new Bright Split Image Range Finder Screen as fitted to current 1994 Rolleiflex 2.8GX. size 56x68mm **£52.00**
Camera screen size 63x68mm to fit older 3.5F, 2.8F Rollei T and Cord Vb **£56.00**
(can not be cut to other sizes)

3.5F and 2.8F light meter kit *(regret no "T" meters)*
Blister packed with instructions, simple to fit **£76.00**
Meter Diffuser white New **£ 8.00**
Scissor Strap Black New **£40.00**
Second-hand scissor strap **£20.00**
Rolleikin complete kit for 3.F, 2.8F Rollei T with case and instructions Almost Mint **£45.00**
Rollei T.L.R. Gold Plated lapel badge **£ 6.00**

Bayonet III

Hinged lens caps new **£12.00**
New B&W Polariser filter (sister company to Rollei) **£68.00**
B&W UV filter **£38.00**
Soft focus 1 or 2 **£45.00**
Orange red ideal for sunsets **£45.00**

Price lists, sample copy of club magazine and club particulars £3.00.
Credit card or cash equivalent in any currency only accepted.

Club Rollei
Jersey Photographic Museum, Hotel de France
St. Saviour's Road, St. Helier, Jersey
Channel Islands, JE2 7LA,
Tel; (0534) 73102 Fax; (0534) 35354

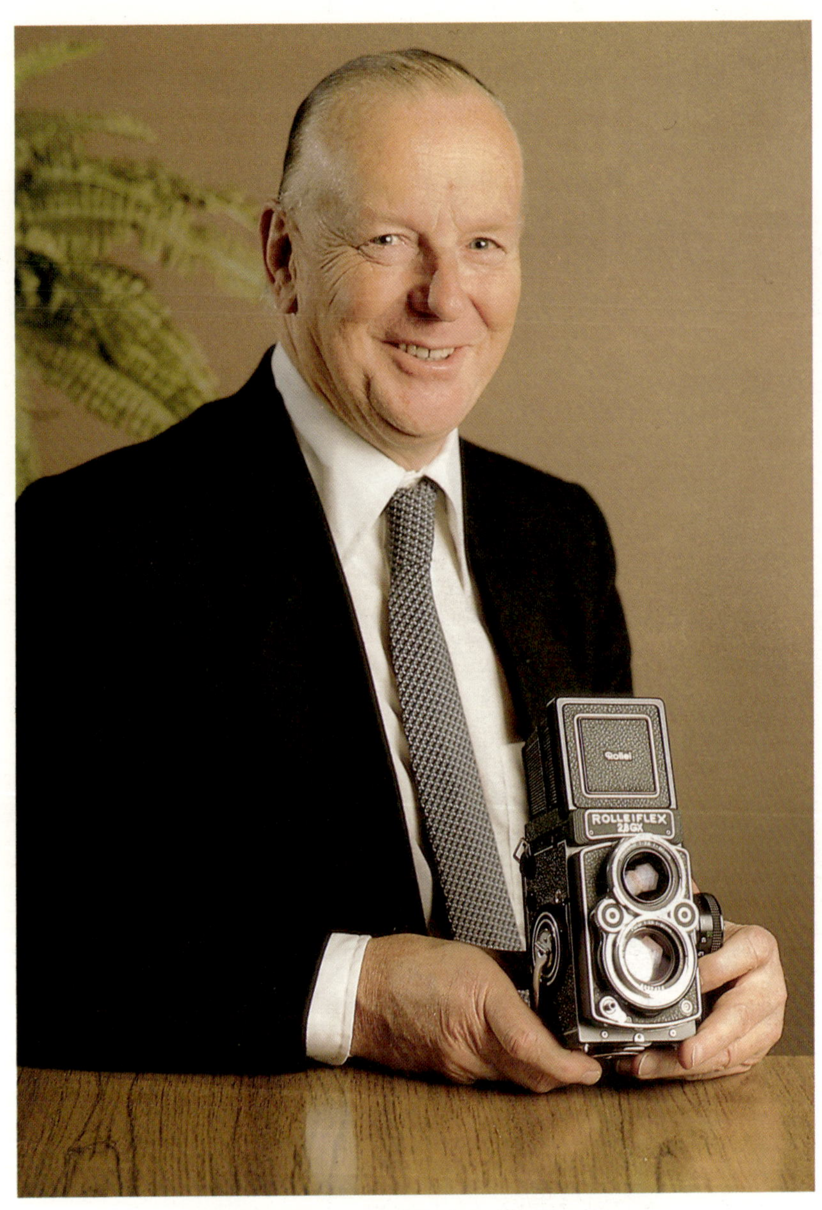

1987 - The Author, Ian Parker, with a first production 2.8GX

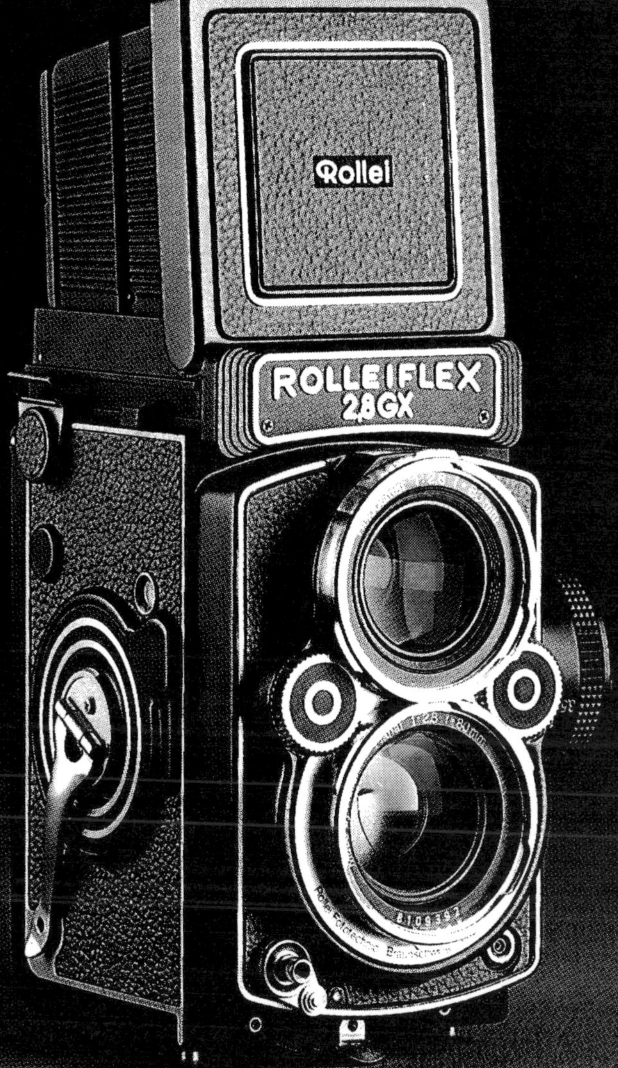

Rollei
ROLLEIFLEX
2,8GX